Rethink
Refuse
Reduce...

Ken Webster
2004

Published by

FSC

BRINGING
ENVIRONMENTAL
UNDERSTANDING TO ALL

FSC Publications

Preston Montford, Shrewsbury SY4 1HW, UK

Occasional Publication 89

ISBN: 978 1 85153 286 5

Acknowledgements

If the philosophers are right then ideas are like birds in a room: we don't so much create them as recognise them. In this long and incomplete process I have been indebted to many people. In particular to my colleague of 20 years Craig Johnson but also to John Huckle, Cherry Duggon (WWF), CSK Consulting (NZ), Peter Edwards, Dr Bill Law, CRAC, Alice Owen, Sarah Wilkinson, Laura Zwingle and Zane Olina (USA). An especial thanks to Caroline Walker (ex-Small School) for her input to a sometimes threadbare patchwork – and for reminding me that watching the Teletubbies is not a crime. Two people in particular took a chance in seeing what potential or otherwise I had and these were Peter Martin from WWF UK and the late Raymond Ryba (University of Manchester).

The production of this publication was funded by Field Studies Council Environmental Education (FSCEE). My thanks go to Dr James Hindson (FSCEE Manager) for his solid support during the preparation of this book and to Janet Jones for keeping track of the details. Some of the materials in this book were originally developed for the environmental education component of the DFID funded 'Roza Vetrov' project in Donetsk, Ukraine, managed by the FSC.

Thanks also go to: Steve Sterling who wrote a helpful formal review of one of the first drafts of the book, Tony Thomas and Liza Ireland who commented on the text; Polyp for illustrations; Deb Oakes for initial cover ideas; Rebecca Farley and Mark Dowding, of FSC Publications, for editing and design; and to all who kindly gave permission for their images to be used in this book.

Contents

Key to symbols

ⓘ Information box

🌍 Case study

Ⳁ Activity

📚 Resource

Foreword

"I am their leader I must follow them" was the cry of the French revolutionary who, looking from his bedroom window, saw the citizen mob chasing down the street. It feels like one of those times now for education for sustainability (ESD). Reality, in the form of changes in society, in the economy and the ecosphere seems to have wrongfooted many of the educators who have set themselves up to offer guidance. The challenges of a consumerist and individualistic culture, rapid globalisation and the clear presence of the effects of global warming, add to increasing inequality and loss of biodiversity. They have shifted the scale of debate and created a new urgency while the outlines of a solar/hydrogen economy and the ecological design movement present new opportunities and demand new learning. The very least we can do is try and keep up.

In the first place there is the need to appreciate the scale of our *unsustainability* and the forces which drive it. It is hard to comprehend how much waste our industrial system creates. Indeed, waste is its primary output. To become sustainable in any meaningful sense requires a revolution in efficiency and a whole rack of systemic changes. To take one element: we would need to produce the same level of output with between a fourth and one tenth of the resources we use today. This isn't something that a save energy campaign, a few recycled bottles or a reusable shopping bag has any purchase on. Indeed, we have been looking down the wrong end of this telescope for decades when it comes to trying to see what matters, and what might make a difference. This insight alone renders trivial much current ESD and environmental education work.

In the second place there is a need to understand, and not dismiss or underplay, the way in which a massively resourced consumer culture has laid claim to the modern mind. The strength of an appeal to restraint and self sacrifice, to a moral stance or even 'community' values – always a standby for schools – is largely bankrupt. Even the UN has begun to recognise that such a message about environment and development has failed. It is worth quoting:

"...the traditional messages from governments and green groups, urging the public to adopt environmentally friendly life-styles and purchasing habits, need to be overhauled."

There is concern that many of these messages are too 'guilt-laden' and disapproving and instead of 'turning people on' to the environment they are switching them off.

Klaus Toepfer, Executive Director of UNEP, said... "Messages from governments, exhorting people to drive their cars less or admonishing them for buying products that cause environmental damage, appear not to be working. People are simply not listening. Making people feel guilty about their life-styles and purchasing habits is achieving only limited success."

Indeed studies indicate that only around 5% of the public in northern countries is embracing so-called sustainable life-styles and sustainable consumerism.

Source:
EarthVision Environmental News
NAIROBI, February 4, 2003

"So we need to look again at how we enlist the public to reduce pollution and live in ways that cause minimal environmental damage. We need to make sustainable life-styles fashionable and 'cool' as young people might say. We also need to make it clear that there are real, personal benefits to living in harmony with the planet", he said.

It seems that not only have we, by and large, been looking at the detail of the symptoms and not the causes, the medicine we have been offering just doesn't work.

In the third place is a more hopeful enterprise. A sustainable, fairer world or something much closer to it can be achieved and the possibilities are exciting. But educators need to understand more of what might underlie it in order to create the vital and interesting lessons and activities that young people need to be able to engage with the thought of sustainability as something aspirational rather than an exercise in belt tightening.

Underlying a 'new industrialism' – as Amory Lovins terms it – are concepts such as (in adult terms) 'ecological design', 'extended producer responsibility'; a shift from 'goods to services' and to 'zero emissions', a switch from taxing people to taxing waste and energy and a move towards a 'solar/hydrogen' economy.

This leads to a fourth place: *renewal*. Democracy has lost most of its clarity and strength – consumer choice seemingly all that is left as a shiny but flawed substitute for self determination. A good consumer is not the same as a good citizen. A sustainable world, in most conceptions, is more diverse, devolved, self reliant and resiliant (a lot like a diverse ecosystem). Renewal may be a long-term gameplan, but it is important and requires informed and critical citizens who are able to motivate themselves and their community to meet their own needs. A part of this renewal is the promotion of more participatory approaches to teaching and learning – and a long, hard look at the messages schools transmit through the ways they are orientated, structured and managed. A sustainable world will not be possible without a quiet revolution in education too, for as Rolf Jucker notes:

"Euro-American education cannot serve as a model for the world. It is saturated with values, ideological concepts and institutional structures which are incompatible with a sustainable society."

This then is the scope of the book: a determined attempt to reorientate ESD towards the challenges of understanding systemic change and towards making sustainability aspirational. It also attempts to bridge, where it can, the gap between progressive ideas about sustainability in theory and in practice.

Rethink, refuse, reduce also acknowledges the simple truth that people learn in different ways and so *it is not a formal text but a collection of stimuli and ideas* (including games, cartoons, photos, maths and online databases) presented around the central arguments.

Ken Webster *Aberystwyth 2004*

66 *The older, wiser environmental movement understands… that the planet cannot be saved by a voluntary change of lifestyle on the part of individuals, but only through collective action – changing laws and economic rules to change people's perception of their short-term self-interest.* **99**

Source: 'For a plant in peril, the future must start in Johannesburg'.
http://news.independent.co.uk/world/environment

Source: Jucker (2002) *Our Common Illiteracy* p238

Chapter 1
The state of the world

66 *The 'boundless' blue sky, the ocean which gives us breath and protects us from the endless black and death, is but an infinitesimally thin film. How dangerous it is to threaten even the smallest part of this gossamer covering, this conserver of life.* **99**
Vladimir Shatalov, COSMONAUT

66 *It is worth noting that (the destruction of the world) is not the work of ignorant people. Rather, it is largely the results of work by people with BAs, BSs, LLBs, MBAs, and PhDs.* **99**
David Orr, PROFESSOR, DEPARTMENT OF ENVIRONMENTAL STUDIES AT OBERLIN COLLEGE, OHIO

To understand what we mean by sustainable development we have to know what it is about our world that is truly *unsustainable*. This may seem an obvious point but often as not too little time is available to help learners understand the roots of unsustainability. This is usually because educators do not fully understand its ramifications themselves. It is in no way their fault; a lack of time and other thieves undermine opportunities for reflecting on our fast-changing and complex world. However, the roots of unsustainability are very deep, affecting almost everything we think and do, but at the same time the need to engage with learners about sustainability is ever more pressing.

One reaction to these twin pressures has been a desire to assume a great deal about where we are and where we are going, to smooth over the complexities and move on to a set of messages for learners; to look at the 'educational small print', as it were. An analogy could be that of a novice hunter setting off into the wilderness with the instructions 'load the rifle, fire it, aim it'. It is nonsense. Yet when it comes to sustainability students are being asked to do just this. In part, this book is a remedy against the 'load-fire-aim' school of thinking.

Human made environmental disaster – Aral Sea
Source: www.stillpictures.com

Good news – the Netherlands government plans ahead to cut...

- carbon dioxide emissions from 12 tonnes per person per year to 4 tonnes in 2010 and 1.7 tonnes in 2030
- freshwater use by 38%
- aluminium consumption by 80%
- timber use by over 60%
- cropland use from 0.45 ha per person to 0.25 ha per person

Increases in the quality of life are to be maintained

Iceland to become the world's first hydrogen economy

Iceland is embarking on a radical plan to abolish the burning of fossil fuels altogether – by transforming itself into the world's first 'hydrogen economy'.

It aims to run all its transport and even its huge fishing fleet on hydrogen produced in Iceland itself. Carbon emissions would fall by over 50%.

Leading spokesman Professor Arnason says: 'People my age will see the beginning. My children will see the transformation. And this will be the energy system when my grandchildren are grown. It's a good vision'.

Source: adapted from a BBC report

The AirGen™ fuel cell generater uses oxygen from air and hydrogen fuel to create electricity. By-products of the reaction are heat and water.

Source: Ballard Power Systems. www.ballard.com

- EU 'take back' regulations are coming into force from 2004 – refrigerators, televisions, washing machines, mobile phones and cars will all be covered eventually – thus encouraging manufacturers to consider how such items are designed and might be disassembled.

- New transport technologies such as hydrogen fuel cells and Negre's compressed air engines (see p. 61) are rapidly being developed – and are already in limited production.

- Congestion charges in London and Oslo have cut congestion by around 25-35% and reduced pollution as fewer vehicles idle or move slowly.

- Following international agreement CFCs have been phased out of industrial use and there is some evidence that the hole in the ozone layer is reducing slowly.

- In Germany labelling of 'eco-products' has increased to over 4100 products in 76 categories.

However, unsustainability isn't just about environment or Nature, it's about social conditions, politics and the economy as well. Increasing wealth has been accompanied by increasing inequality, both within nations and regions and in the world as a whole and with this comes poverty and many serious health and welfare issues. In richer nations wealth has been accompanied by increasing crime, drug and alcohol abuse, mental health problems, and the so-called diseases of affluence such as cancer and heart disease.

In the poorer countries problems are more obvious. The number of people in the developing world who...

- Subsist on less than $1 per day is **1.3 billion**
- Lack access to safe drinking water is **1.3 billion**
- Lack access to health services is **0.9 billion**
- Are living with HIV/AIDS is **28.5 million**
- Lack access to sanitation is **2.6 billion**
- Lack access to electric power services is **2.0 billion**

Note: As of 1998, the total population of developing countries was approximately 4.58 billion.

Sources: UNDP 1996, UNDP 2000 UNDP *et al* 2001

Here is how wealth is distributed globally.

Source: Polyp

 1.3

To have and have not

- 5% of the world's human population resides in the USA
- 30% of the world's resources are used by the USA
- 8 motor vehicles are on the roads in China for every 1,000 citizens
- 750 motor vehicles are on the roads in the USA for every 1,000 citizens
- 15 kilograms of paper are consumed annually by each person in the developing world
- 333 kilograms of paper are consumed annually by each person in the USA
- 20% of the world's population lives in industrialized nations
- 75% of the world's pollutants and waste are produced by industrialized nations
- 8 billion dollars are spent each year on cosmetics in the USA
- 9 billion dollars would be needed each year (in addition to current expenditures) to provide water and sanitation for all people in developing nations

Collated by Josh Sevin for GRIST Magazine.

Sources: (1,2) Earth Communications Office; (3-7) World Resources Institute; (8) Earth Communications Office; (9,10) Worldwatch Institute.

It is a cruelly familiar world of excess and destitution combined. This can be further illustrated by taking a closer look at the leading nation when it comes to excess and waste – the USA and comparing it to other nations or groups. Some way behind the USA come the major European economies and Japan.

No satisfaction should be taken from the choice of a USA example. All over the world consumption patterns have tended to follow the USA as income rises. As the following cartoon illustrates, over-consumption is usually seen as the evil of the 'other fellow'.

More discussion of consumption can be found in Chapters 2 and 3.

Source: Polyp

The problem is worldwide and really quite fundamental. Resources – materials and energy – are being used faster than they can be replaced. Some resources are non-renewable. Most resources are being used by the richest nations for the benefit of a minority of their populations. The economy is chronically inefficient and wastes are increasing to levels which affect the very integrity of the ecosphere upon which all of humankind depends. One of the examples most often quoted is the impact of rising levels of carbon dioxide and other 'greenhouse' gases on the world's climate.

The case study of China (1.4) brings into focus just how close the world might be to the limits of its productive capacity and of its ability to deal with wastes. The Chinese population is so large that even small increases in consumption will bring severe problems. And China might well argue that it deserves to increase its consumption...

1.4

Some learners might resist the logic of this form of presentation because they need to 'prove it to themselves'. This can be done in a number of ways. One of the simplest is to let learners juggle with the variables themselves.

Unsustainable equation?

The 'environmental impact' (**i**) the world experiences depends on a number of variables. First there is the number of people: 'Population' (**p**). Then there is how much each person consumes: 'Consumption' (**c**). Last there is 'Technology' (**t**) or how efficiently resources are used (another way of putting this is the extra waste produced in providing the next unit of consumption). This gives a simple equation:

i = c x p x t

Imagine that environmental impact stays the same in 2050 as it is now. Of course most people would wish it to fall, but this is just an example...

Imagine consumption continues to increase in the way it has. This means it doubles every 25-30 years if it is growing at 2-3% a year. This is a reasonable assumption. So a conservative estimation puts consumption in 2050 at about three times greater than consumption in 2003.

Population is growing too. Although it is not growing as fast as it once did, the population could still grow half as much again by 2050. Remembering that the idea is that '**i**' should stay the same... the only real variable left in the equation is '**t**' or how *efficiently* humanity behaves when using resources.

What will '**t**' have to be in 2050 to 'balance the books'?

It could be done in percentages. Let **i** = 100% or the 'index' at year 2003 so the aim is to make sure that does not change...

i = c x p x t
so in 2050...

1.4

If China...

- If each of China's 1.2 billion people were to consume one extra chicken per *year*, and if that chicken were to be raised primarily on grain, this would account for as much grain as all the annual grain exports of Canada, the world's second largest exporter.

- If China were to consume seafood at Japan's per capita rate, it would need 100 million tons, more than today's total catch.

- If China were to match the US for per capita car ownership and oil consumption, it would need more than today's global output of oil, and its cars would emit roughly as much CO_2 as from all the world's transportation today.

- If China consumed wood and wood products at the Japanese rate their demand would exceed Japan's nine times over.

Source: Quoted in The century ahead: Ever greater problems or ever wider opportunities? Prof N Myers in Environmental Awareness Vol. 24, No 4, 2001, India

1.5

Balancing the books

Whatever we set **i** to be, the other side of the equation will have to work out the same to keep **i** steady.

100 = 300 (the increase in consumption) x 150 (the increase in population) x $\frac{1}{450}$

(i) 1.6

Why 1/450?

If we re-arrange the equation...

$t = \dfrac{i}{c \times p}$ $t = \dfrac{100}{300 \times 150}$ $t = \dfrac{1}{450}$

66 *In the real world relatively few politicians can contemplate enforcing birth control and even fewer reducing consumption. 'Eco-efficiency' in all its forms looks like the only short- and medium-term political game in town. Educators need to recognise this explicitly.* **99**

Why 1/450? Technology (**t**) will have to be 450% more efficient to counter the effects of increasing consumption and population (i.e. balance the equation) That means between four and five times more efficient so everything will have to be made with between a **quarter** and a **fifth** of the resources which it takes now. It will take more than switching a few lights off and a recycling campaign to achieve this. It will require a quiet revolution in how resources are used. Many educators have never really grasped the magnitude of the change required and for them this equation is a powerful wake-up call.

Let learners imagine what scenarios they like and vary **i**, **c**, **p** and **t** – 'balancing the books' always comes out as a *very* difficult task. If there was a demand that environmental impact (**i**) should *fall* – perhaps because humanity is *already* beyond safe limits in its effects on the ecosphere, as has been argued earlier – then the task is even harder.

The **i = c x p x t** exercise may be a little too abstract for some learners. Another more popular attempt to make the nature of unsustainability 'visible' is called 'eco-footprints'. It translates consumption into the area of the earth's surface needed to provide the resources and waste sinks which match this consumption. It's an excellent tool, computer software can be used to manage the calculations to provide instant feedback on personal 'footprints'. More details can be found on page 13.

'Y' Ecological Footprints

One of the first problems for an ESD programme is making the *unsustainable* nature of our lifestyles 'visible' to students and adults alike. The *ecological footprint* is a way of doing this. WWF, the global environment network, uses this method in its annual publication the *Living Planet Report*. Here's how they explain it.

The Ecological Footprint (EF) is a measure of the consumption of renewable natural resources by a human population, be it that of a country, a region or the whole world. A population's EF is the total area of productive land or sea required to produce all the crops, meat, seafood, wood and fibre it consumes, to sustain its energy consumption and to give space for its infrastructure. The EF can be compared with the biologically productive capacity of the land and sea available to that population.

The Earth has about 11.4 billion hectares of productive land and sea space, after all unproductive areas of icecaps, desert and open ocean are discounted, or about a quarter of its surface area. Divided between the global population of six billion people, this total equates to just 1.9 hectares per person. While the EF of the average African or Asian consumer was less than 1.4 hectares per person in 1999, the average Western European's footprint was about 5.0 hectares, and the average North American's was about 9.6 hectares.

The EF of the world average consumer in 1999 was 2.3 hectares per person, or 20% above the earth's biological capacity of 1.90 hectares per person. In other words, humanity now exceeds the planet's capacity to sustain its consumption of renewable resources. We are able to maintain this global overdraft on a temporary basis by eating into the earth's capital stocks of forest, fish and fertile soils. This is not sustainable in the long-term – the only sustainable solution is to live within the biologically productive capacity of the earth.

However, current trends are moving humanity away from achieving this minimum requirement for sustainability, not towards it. The global ecological footprint has grown from about 70% of the planet's biological capacity in 1961 to about 120% of its biological capacity in 1999. Furthermore, future projections based on likely scenarios of population growth, economic development and technological change, show that humanity's footprint is increasing.

Source: http://www.panda.org/news_facts/publications/general/livingplanet/index.cfm

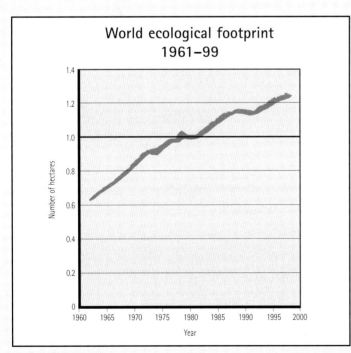

World ecological footprint 1961–99

Number of hectares (y-axis)
Year (x-axis)

Source Bestfootforward.com

FSC

Resources

A comprehensive ecological footprints calculator is available online (**http://www.earthday.net/footprint/index.asp**)

Once logged on, moving the mouse over the appropriate part of the world map will give a range of choices for study: all the major nations and language options are here. Students or participants then complete the simple stage-by-stage quiz and receive footprint data in hectares relevant to themselves and the country they have chosen. This is automatically compared to the average available per person in the world. The result is also measured against the number of planets which would be necessary if everyone consumed at that calculated rate. It is a sobering thought.

The footprint calculation has several categories: food, mobility, shelter and goods/services. Depending on whether the work is with colleagues or students each of these categories might be the basis for fruitful discussion using starter questions such as:

• *How could I change my activities to reduce the impact?*

• *What could government do to reduce our impact?*

• *What could business do to reduce its impact*

• *What new technologies or systems could help reduce our impact?*

• *What incentives and disincentives could assist in reducing my/our impact?*

• *How do we compare to other countries? Should we care about the answers anyway?*

• *"It's not us who consumes too much!" Compared to whom? EU or USA or ...?*

• *Does development mean more consumption or a better quality of life? Are the two always related?*

• *'Ecologically sustainable' means ...?*

Follow up

Students and participants might be given extracts from the *Living Planet Report 2000* such as the following comparison between the UK, Russia and the Ukraine.

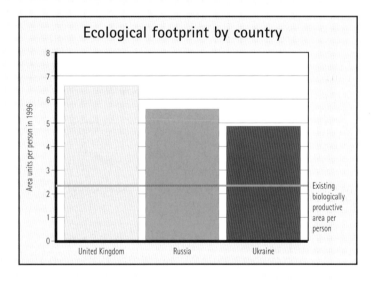

An interesting discussion can be had from comparing the average footprint of Russia and the UK (which is broadly similar) with the quality of life (which is not the same). The UK may show evidence of improved resource efficiency leading to a higher quality of life.

If used in a workshop for teaching colleagues a number of further questions might be discussed:

- Is ecological footprinting a useful idea?

- What do we expect students to gain from it?

- Is it still too much 'doom and gloom?'

- What is the positive side of ecological footprinting?

Weblinks

Downloadable software (English language)
http://csf.concord.org

Uses and applications of ecological footprinting
http://www.rprogress.org

Comparing different nations
http://www.ecouncil.ac.cr/rio/focus/report/english/footprint

It's the system stupid

66 Growth for the sake of growth. notes environmental writer Edward Abbey, is the ideology of the cancer cell. Just as a continually growing cancer eventually destroys its life support system by destroying its host, a continuously expanding global economy is destroying its host. 99

Some educators have successfully used games or simulations to illustrate unsustainability and this aspect of the 'bigger picture'. In the downloadable resources section (see **http://www.efseurope.org**) there is an extremely well-known activity know as the *Trade Game*. It has been carefully adapted here to illustrate some of the ways in which unsustainability is built into the 'rules of the game' – the ways in which the dominant interests of the world conducts business and commerce and how these draw others in. It is an extraordinarily powerful activity and works for all groups above about 12 in number and from age 10 years upwards, including adults.

An unsustainable world is clearly not some kind of accident. Nor something regrettable like a train crash or forgetting to feed the dog. Nor is it, as some naively believe, a moral lapse – a consequence of a few 'greedy' people or individuals not choosing 'green' products, not taking the bus or recycling their Coca Cola bottles in suburbia.

ⓘ 1.7
Test your knowledge...

What do these acronyms stand for?
What do these organisations do?

WTO • OECD • G7 • IBRD • WEF

Answers on p. 94.

> 66 *Perverse subsidies (e.g. in agriculture, mining, road transport, oil and gas, nuclear energy) at $1.5 trillion are twice as large as global military spending per year; larger than the annual sales of the top 12 corporations and larger than the global expenditure in the fossil fuels industry or the global insurance industry.* 99

> 66 *More than $600 billion a year of taxpayers' money is spent by governments to subsidize deforestation, overfishing, the burning of fossil fuels, the use of virgin raw materials and other environmentally destructive activities.* 99

Prof N Myers

The *Trade Game* illustrates the existence of vested interests – that many people exploit the rules of the game as they exist and wish to continue to do so. In the real world the current rules of world trade have a huge impact on the prospects for sustainability. It is neglected by many educators and learners alike or dealt with only in outline, as a 'development' issue (which, sadly often equates with 'over the horizon and out of sight').

It is perhaps seen as too 'political' or just too complicated, but the enormous barrier of vested interests to achieving sustainability can be illuminated by these quotations on government subsidies from Professor Myers (see left).

Removing subsidies of this scale as Myers has argued represents *the single most important change that would help bring a more sustainable world*, yet it is equally arguable that this theme is the *least* discussed of all possible sustainability themes in pre-18 education. Chapter 2 has more to say on the curious world of priorities in ESD.

The weblinks and further reading give access to more on 'globalisation' in general and this book includes just a couple of workshop stimulus pieces designed to encourage a debate about issues associated with how the world economy has evolved (see Appendix II and the Data area in **http://www.efseurope.org**).

Other workshop stimuli which might run well alongside or instead of the *Trade Game* are *Coffee: Sun or Shadee* (p. 17) or *Bananas*, based on an excellent *JustBiz* resource (see **http://www.efseurope.org**). The use of case studies around individual commodities, poverty and development is more common in formal education than a theoretical approach. It can be a helpful entree to global issues of trade and sustainability.

⊕ Coffee – sun or shade?

A nice cup of coffee. Maybe an expensive cup of coffee if it's from Starbucks or Coffee Republic. At supermarkets the price of coffee on the shelves has been steady for five years yet few people comment on it or know that the price of coffee beans, the raw material has been in decline for most of these years. It is at levels at which real hardship is being faced by the grower and his or her workers. In addition the shift from coffee grown in traditional ways – in the shade of the forest – to coffee grown in the sun has had significant environmental impacts. This activity tries to get behind the coffee market to make sense of these bare facts.

⊤ Aim

- To promote critical thinking in the context of information about the coffee market
- To explore the question – what would fair trade in coffee mean?
- To explore the relationship between technology and supply and demand in primary products
- To compare shade- and sun-grown coffee on environmental and social grounds

Resources (p. 19-22)

1.1 Coffee markets (data and growers' story)

1.2 From tree to cup (data)

1.3 Shade and sun compared

1.4 Quotes

Access to the internet or printouts of material from the sites listed, as necessary.

Method

Since coffee is a widely consumed product, ascertain what learners know about its price, the types of coffee available, where it comes from and why coffee is more expensive in some cafes/stalls/shops than others. This perhaps relates to differing overheads – including rent, staff costs, the investment in fixtures and fittings as well as the characteristics of the clientele and the choice of coffee available. Assert that a kilo of ground coffee on a supermarket shelf in 1998 cost around $26US (£17) in the UK. Ask students to find out what the price is now. Using the original data, estimate the price paid for the approximately 3 kilograms of coffee beans which are needed to produce a kilogram of ground and roasted coffee. Learners will tend to overestimate. The approximate price is 42 cents (say, 30 pence). Introduce the resources in ⧉ 1.1-1.4. Discuss the information enclosed.

- *Is too much 'profit' being made?*
- *By whom?*
- *What about the costs involved?*
- *Why has price fallen since 1997?*
- *Why the shift away from shade-grown coffee?*

Task: Using the internet resource indicated in Weblinks, learners write their own story of what has happened to the growers and how the trade might be made fairer for them and less damaging to the environment in production areas.

Or...

Task: If coffee bean prices doubled (to give growers a better return) what would happen to the final price? Would you as a customer pay the extra if you knew it was going to the grower? What would happen in the world market if prices for beans went up?

Or...

Task: Using ⧉ 1.3 compare and contrast sun-grown and shade-grown coffee. Explain the decline in shade-grown coffee and identify those aspects of coffee production which are not 'costed.'

Commentary

Growers would benefit in the short term from a price rise tied to growers' returns. Perhaps most customers would accept a price rise in the supermarket of 9 cents (6p) a kilogram out of a final (1998) price of $26 (£17). This represents a third of one percent rise. Rising bean prices in the real world of an unregulated global market (consisting of many suppliers but stagnating demand) and few buyers would encourage even more production thus leading to falling prices in the medium term unless unsold beans were stockpiled to absorb the surplus. This is an expensive procedure. Who would finance it? Over-production has come through increased competition and the adoption of more intensive production methods – the so called 'sun grown' coffee. These methods damage wildlife, convert more land to coffee production, damage land fertility and are unsustainable in the long run.

Another issue raised by ⬙ 1.2 is that of appropriate returns. The coffee drinking experience may start with coffee but it is clear that the bulk of the costs are in the retail end of the chain: customers expect city-centre outlets, comfy chairs, and, to catch their attention – advertising. High overheads of investment in premises and wages are the result. It is not clear that exhorbitant profits *are* being made anywhere in the chain. A very difficult issue. Who's the bad guy?

Even if those consumers aware of the problems demand more 'fair trade' and shade-grown coffee then this niche market is currently around 1-2% of the total market for coffee.

Sustainable?

The big question... Learners might be asked to consider the ways in which coffee growers could be helped to simultaneously achieve *a better quality of life* and a reduction of *coffee growing's impact on the environment*. In doing so they might begin to engage in discussion about the 'rules of trade' and how they are set; about the way prices (in adult language) do or do not reflect full social and environmental costs, and the effects of an imbalance of power between the different parties in world trade. All these are important factors in understanding the *unsustainable* world. Learners might fail to answer the question set – if it were easy to answer then poverty amongst coffee growers and workers could be significantly reduced, and quickly – but at least in engaging in the debate, in probing ideas such as 'quality of life' or 'environmental impact' or the 'balance of trade' they will have clarified their thinking. As Einstein once noted:

❝ *The mere formulation of a problem is far more essential than its solution, which may be merely a matter of mathematical or experimental skills. To raise new questions, new possibilities, to regard old problems from a new angle requires creative imagination and marks real advances in science.* ❞

(NB: Chapter 5 deals in more detail with the importance of raising new questions as part of changing teaching and learning styles – a key element of education for sustainable development.)

1.1: Coffee market

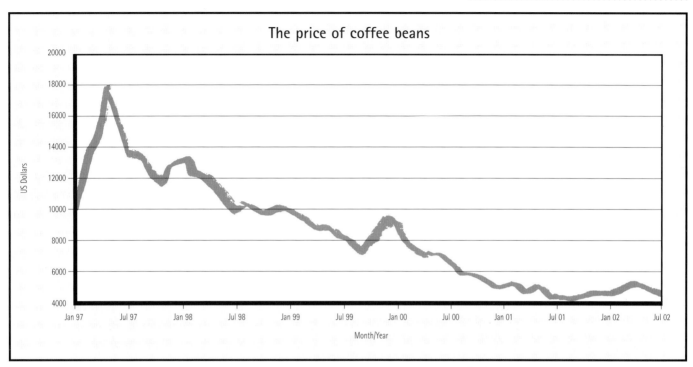

The price of coffee beans

US Dollars

20000
18000
16000
14000
12000
10000
8000
6000
4000

Jan 97   Jul 97   Jan 98   Jul 98   Jan 99   Jul 99   Jan 00   Jul 00   Jan 01   Jul 01   Jan 02   Jul 02

Month/Year

The price of coffee beans based on ICO composite indicator price (green coffee). Monthly averages January 1997–July 2002

" This situation is caused by the current imbalance between supply and demand for coffee. Total production in coffee year 2001/02 is estimated at around 113 million bags (60kg bags) while world consumption is just over 106 million bags. On top of that, world stocks amount to some 40 million bags. Coffee production has been rising at an average annual rate of 3.6%, but demand has been increasing by only 1.5%. At the origin of this coffee glut lies the rapid expansion of production in Vietnam and new plantations in Brazil, which is harvesting a record crop in the current season... **"**

Source: International Coffee Organisation report

📖 1.2: From tree to cup

A USA coffee roaster reports on his business costs (1998)

Columbian Supremo green beans	$1.30 per lb*
Transport in, storage, handling	$0.11
18% loss of weight during roasting equiv. to	$0.31
Fuel for roasting	$0.12
Packing into 5lb bags	$0.25
Shipping out	$0.30
Total	**$2.39**
Overheads for roaster and distributor (mortgages, machinery, bank charges, repairs insurances, sales commissions)	$2.15
Profits	$0.24 (5%)
Total: to reach specialist shop	**$4.78**
Shop costs (rent, wages, overheads, etc) + 'reasonable' profits	$3.22-5.20
Total: to reach customer, including profit	**$8-10**

*(fluctuates wildly)

If supplied to "*a coffee house outlet the proprietor converts the $4.78 per pound beans into regular coffee at $1 a cup, and capuccino or latte for $2 or more. If the proprietor gets 40 cups per pound that translates to an outrageous $40-$80 a pound for coffee in beverage form, minus the cost of milk etc. On the other hand coffee house owners have to pay astronomical rents and allow customers to hog a table for long philosphical conversations or solitary reading over their single cup of coffee... coffee house owners may be working 15hr days, six days a week, fighting the health inspector and the Starbucks just opened down the street.*"

NB: To convert US pounds to kilograms – 1lb=0.45kg.

Source: Figures sourced from p. 330
Uncommon Grounds by Mark Pendergrast,
Texere, London 2001

1.3: Shade and sun compared

A shift towards plantation coffee has increased. Here is a comparison of the two approaches to coffee growing.

Comparing **shade grown** (forest) coffee with **sun grown** (plantation) coffee

	Shade	**Sun**
Yield	Lower (~25-40%)	Higher
Coffee plants per hectare	1000-2000	3000-7000
Kilograms per hectare per year	550	1600
Lifetime of coffee plants	24-30 years	12-15 years
Number of other crops	High	Low/none
Flavour	Less bitter	More bitter
Producer	Mostly small-scale growers	Mostly large-scale growers
Number of bird species	150	20-50
Proportion of (birds) avifauna in normal forest	66%	10%
Number of mid-sized mammal species	24	Almost none
Number of other animal species	More ants, beetles, epiphytes, amphibians, and other species	Fewer ants, beetles, epiphytes, amphibians, and other species
Weeding	Lower	Higher
Chemical fertilizers	Lower	Higher
Pesticides	Lower	Higher
Irrigation	Lower	Higher
Soil erosion	Lower	Higher
Soil acidification	Lower	Higher
Toxic runoff	Lower	Higher

Source: www.seattleaudubon.org

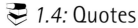 *1.4:* Quotes

> " Ten years ago the world coffee economy was worth $30 billion, of which producers received $12 billion. Today it is worth $50 billion, with producers receiving just $8 billion. "

Source: *The Guardian*

> " In last decade, the major coffee companies' revenues have doubled. During the same time, the earnings of ordinary coffee farmers have been slashed by two-thirds. "

Nestor Osorio, Executive Director, International Coffee Organization

> " It is estimated that over 125 million people worldwide are dependent on coffee for their livelihoods. But since it is a perennial crop it is not easy to switch to an alternative when prices are at today's levels. The consequences of the current situation vary but in many cases prices do not even cover the costs of production. "

International Coffee Organization report

> " At the same time, the World Bank and its cousin, the Asian Development Bank, gave generous loans to Vietnam to plant huge amounts of low-quality robusta coffee. 'Vietnam has become a successful producer,' said Don Mitchell, principal economist at the World Bank. 'In general, we consider it to be a huge success.'
>
> Although Mitchell acknowledges the damage to nations that cannot compete with Vietnam's $1-per-day labour costs or Brazil's mechanized plantations – such as Guatemala, with its $3-per-day minimum wage – he said the losers must switch to farming other crops. "

Source: Mourning coffee by Robert Collier,
San Francisco Chronicle 2001
www.seattleaudubon.org/shadecoffee

Weblinks

Understanding the coffee trade: a growers story
http://www.independent.co.uk/
http://www.globalexchange.org/economy/coffee

Extensive coffee data
http://www.ico.org/

More about 'shade' coffee
http://www.seattleaudubon.org/

The state of the world: summary

Unsustainability, it seems, is built into the working of our world. But many international bodies such as the World Trade Organisation, the World Bank, most governments and industry bodies believe that the basic rules of free trade and the pursuit of economic growth *will help bring* sustainable development, providing it is managed responsibly. The argument is that the medicine works, we have only to adjust the dose and manage the side effects. Sustainability becomes quite a simple idea: Its 'business as usual, but greener'. Many would want to add the phrase '...and fairer' but yet others would simply disagree altogether, insisting that the problems caused by modern day capitalism cannot be solved the same way.

Source: Polyp

Different ideas reflect different interests but also quite different *philosophies* – different 'world-views.' An education for sustainable development therefore needs to look not only at the *State of the World* but also at our *State of Mind.*

Chapter 2
State of mind I

❝ *The theory determines what we observe.* **❞**
Albert Einstein

❝ In 1543, Copernicus published a paper arguing that the Sun did not revolve around the Earth, but that the Earth revolved around the Sun, producing a new world-view. Today we are in need of a similar shift in thinking about the relationship between the Earth and the economy. Economists argue that the environment is a subset of the economy.

But in reality, the economy is a subset of environment, of the Earth's ecosystem. Sustaining economic progress depends on restructuring the economy according to the principles of ecology, making it compatible with the Earth's ecosystem. **❞**
Lester R. Brown. *Eco-Economy: Building an Economy for the Earth*

World-views matter, Einstein was right. Our mental models, our assumptions about how the world works lie very deep and they shape our thoughts, even to the extent that what we 'observe' is framed by these models. It is worth a slight detour to understand how. Our modern outlook has been heavily influenced by the Enlightenment – and Copernicus was at the beginnings of it. Here science cast light on a world which had hitherto been but a mysterious dispensation of God, though woven with finest subtlety, all things to their place.

To the now 'enlightened' individual the route to understanding things was by taking them apart, to find the atoms or fundamental parts. Moreover, the universe, after Newton and Descartes, was now assumed to run like a clock, according to fixed, but discernible rules. Thus these parts related together like cogs in a machine which could with mathematical precision be made to act to our will. All was under the preview of Man and the world was now a wild, insensitive, godless place set before Man for his purposes.

God remained a matter of the individual conscience: all else could be *engineered*. Resources into machines and goods, people into citizens, and perhaps, as Marx believed, the eventual but inevitable triumph of the proletariat. Heaven could be created on earth if only the *mechanism* could be found. An intoxicating sense of endless progress; of lifting the common people from their superstitions and ignorance, of newer and better technologies, of abundance such that all human needs would be met and, who knows, Man could dream of travel in space...

This then was the mindset of the industrial age and it is still with us: that sense of alienation from Nature, but with the aspiration to control it, the focus on the individual, on material progress and development through the rules science has uncovered. It is not surprising that the economy of the industrial age looks a little like a machine – converting resources into goods by instruction of the market (once again the *mechanism* appeared to have been discovered).

It's an *idea* first and foremost, a useful one, but like all ideas just an approximation of reality. This mechanistic idea has profound consequences since it assumes that what matters has a price and that markets send accurate messages through prices. This is a key insight for a number of reasons, all of them acutely relevant to education and sustainability. Firstly there is the idea that somehow the economy is running according to rules which are 'given': a part of how the world works. As a former UK prime minister once said "you can't buck the market." Secondly, there is the idea that this economy produces stuff we want (since the consumer *demands* it...) but with some leftover wastes (i.e. since it works efficiently in our service then pollution is just a minor problem which has to be weighed against material progress) Thirdly, the idea that applying these successes to other parts of the world will bring the same benefits – although there will be problems – for example rising third world populations and corrupt governments.

Perceptions matter. A more realistic image of the economy is of a waste producing economy. Literally, most of what it 'produces' is waste: this is the consequence of the economic rules which value somethings but not others – it also produces some useful goods and services but almost as a by-product 'take it-make it-dump it' is an accurate description of its main activity.

FSC

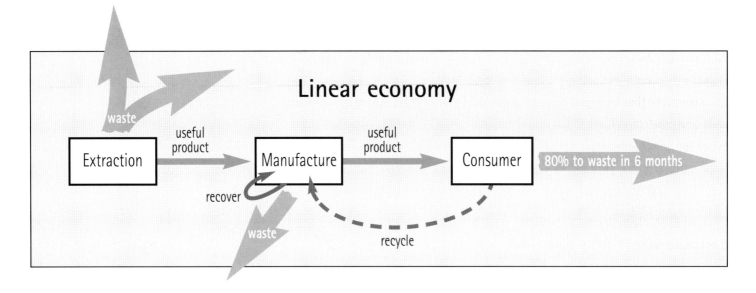

Linear economy

Extraction → useful product → Manufacture → useful product → Consumer → 80% to waste in 6 months

waste

recover

waste

recycle

> ❝...around 50% of all materials used and moved by mankind cannot be recycled.❞
>
> Rolf Jucker (2002) *Our Common Illiteracy* p93

> ❝...about 93% of the materials we buy and consume never end up in saleable products at all. Moreover, 80% of products are discarded after a single use, many of the rest are not as durable as they should be.❞
>
> Lovins *et al* (1998) *Factor Four*

> ❝ Systems without feedback are, by definition, stupid. But systems with feedback of even the most rudimentary sort can grow smarter in a hurry. How clean a car would you buy if its exhaust pipe, instead of being aimed at pedestrians, fed directly into the passenger compartment?❞
>
> Lovins *et al* (1998) *Factor Four*

Already in this simple and partial shift of perception are clues as to why many educational attempts at understanding the general issue of sustainability fail – they do not have a sense of the sheer volume of material and waste involved and therefore no realistic sense of what changes are required to qualify anything for the tag 'sustainable' or, for that matter, how much the rules of economics are a partial but convenient fiction.

The first two quotations (left) pretty much frame the issue.

Another way of describing the linear economy is to say that there is very little in the way of *feedback*, of flows of materials and resources back into the system, which means it is a 'dumb' approach. As teachers and learners know, feedback – *interaction* – is an essential feature of any intelligent learning environment.

Again and again it is our perceptions which are most challenged when it comes to sustainability.

To be fair, there is a kind of intelligence (feedback) in our 'waste economy'. Trading, the interplay of supply and demand is a feedback loop: it gives information to buyers and sellers. Trading has become very sophisticated and is based on prices of course. What matters to the market has a price. This has become so important an idea that *value* itself has become confused with *price* since nothing very important, it is assumed, will exist outside of a market. Just as in the public mind 'more' has become the same as 'better', *price* has become *value*.

As the environmental services provided by the ecosphere (cleaning air, regulating oxygen levels, the water cycle, ensuring biodiversity, etc.) generally have no price they have no obvious value as either a resource or as a waste sink and they are literally invisible to the *idea* of material Progress. And Progress has been very successful, at least for what is seen as 'the golden billion', that 20% of the world's population who owns so much.

66*As an exercise Robert Costanza of the University of Maryland calculated the approximate value in money terms of all the environmental services the planet provides. Although hardly precise – that's not the point – it came out around 33 trillion dollars or about twice the value of the world's economic output for 1997.***99**

Source: *Nature* May 15 1997

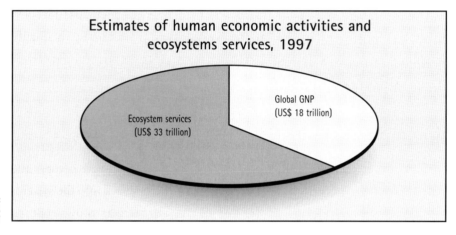

Estimates of human economic activities and ecosystems services, 1997

Global GNP
(US$ 18 trillion)

Ecosystem services
(US$ 33 trillion)

Source:
tanza et al.
1997

Essentially we are discussing perceptions or myths about how the world works and any education for sustainable development has to engage in *ideas* more than issues for issues, in the real world usually derive from the application of certain world-views, or dominant myths. ⓘ 2.1 uncovers these in more detail.

ⓘ 2.1

Challenging the dominant myths

Professor Rolf Jucker writes on unsustainable thinking ...the mass media, the public relations industry on the payroll of business interests, official politics, but also university and other education the world over still promote, almost unchallenged, the dominant myths[*] ...which are the driving motors behind perpetuating our unsustainable present:

- Any mainstream media reports on the economy still equate growth of the GNP with good news, even though we know that within a finite, materially non-growing system, such as the earth, the only sustainable option is zero growth, quite apart from the fact that the GNP has long been discredited as a serious measure of human welfare.

- Linear material and scientific-technological progress is still seen as a blessing to humankind, even though we know that most of the technological 'progress' brought about by the industrial and now electronic revolution is unsustainable in terms of the excessive materials and energy consumption in the long run. There are, in fact, very few technologies and procedures of modern life which stand up to a sustainable life-cycle and impact test.

- The 'development model', i.e. the assumption that there is a linear, necessary and positive progression from 'barbaric', 'uncivilised' and 'undeveloped' indigenous peoples to the American way of life, has long been shown to be absurd, for two main reasons: first, if, as implied, all people on earth should lead American lifestyles, we would need at least another four planet earths to provide the resources for this endeavour; second, the idea is in effect totalitarian: it assumes that the Western lifestyle is the only valid one and that all other ways of living have to be destroyed. Yet this outdated idea of development is still at the heart of the... world trade agenda.

[*]Sometimes called 'metanarratives' – deeply held 'stories' about how the world works.

Source: Rolf Jucker (2002)

Leeds Postcard: LP544 *Perestoika* by Pete Betts, first published in 1990

❝ I *shop* therefore I am. **❞**

Perhaps the most pervasive of all the ideas of the modern age is *consumerism*. It has been quite simply revolutionary – '*I shop therefore I am*' was a 20th century revision of Descartes' famous phrase '*I think therefore I am*'.

When the Berlin Wall fell in 1989 Pete Betts, a satirist, summed up the situation. The arm of Lenin is seen pointing, not as in the classic Soviet posters of the early 20th century, to the frontlines of the proletarian revolution but to the West, adorned with a large branded supermarket bag. 'Go shopping'.

According to some commentators, Soviet style state socialism failed because it had not been able to match the economic growth of the West. It was not so much freedom that was demanded but a freedom and an opportunity to consume more. Although this is a controversial idea it is not controversial to say that consumerism is the dominant idea in an increasingly material world. As an idea it is based on the simple identity: more equals better (and therefore more means happier) And happier refers, principally, to me the individual. The cartoon (below left) pokes fun at our uncritical attitude to consumerism.

As an *idea* it is possibly the greatest challenge of all the challenges facing sustainability. For clarity try and look at it in reverse. If:

less = worse

then

worse = less happiness.

Who will vote for it? Who wants an unhappier life? Yet, naively, much education for sustainable development wags a moral finger and effectively ignores the most significant world trend of the industrial age and assumes that for the 'love of the planet' or of 'community' and 'acting as a good citizen' then the majority of people, young and old will choose to reduce their consumption. Some chance! Solid research suggests that only about 5% will contemplate such a path.

2.2

ESD can't just be about the committed 'green' but it often has that connotation.

Beauty and the beast?

Source: © David Woodfall / stillpictures www.stillpictures.com

Perhaps even more than an examination of the *State of the World* an examination of the dominant myths of consumerism is the key resource for an educator interested in sustainable development issues. Yet it is almost never taught – at least not as something that needs to be understood rather than just condemned, or, as is more likely, quietly ignored. Some writers like Ingolfur Blühdorn go even further and suggest that we are fooling ourselves, that deep down what most of us want is to be seen to be concerned, to do a little bit to salve our consciences and laud tokenistic efforts at sustainability while hanging on to our material gains.

ⓘ
2.2

66 *The unsustainability of the contemporary frame of mind is not just one of its curable faults, but an essential feature. The hypothesis is that the contemporary frame of mind has no genuine appreciation for the ecologist goals of social justice and ecological integrity, and that the discourse of sustainability may have to be interpreted as a strategy to disguise an unsustainability that late modern societies neither can, nor really want to, remove.* 99

Ingolfur Blühdorn, University of Bath

It seems we are green and aware of social issues until it comes to paying for it.

ⓘ **2.2**

The green consumer

"The research shows that, despite substantial growth in their financial power, ethical consumers still command only a small share of these markets. The basket of household goods claims the biggest share of the cake, with 5.4% of relevant sales in 2000. Other products and services barely register..." *Cooperative Society report* see http://www.greenconsumerguide.com/features/ethical_purchasingindex2001.pdf

"...apart from a small minority of exceptionally committed green consumers, the mass of the market does not want green products if it means paying more."

...several studies show that the social or environmental characteristics of the product are the most important purchasing criteria for only about 5-10% of this market."

Source: *The green challenge – the market for eco-friendly products* Prof Paul Stoneman, *et al* Warwick Business School

This is the end point of an exploration of the roots of our state of mind: a sense that we are so wedded to the mindset of a modern world that we even deny that we are. In ESD the challenge may be to find ways of uncovering this mindset, of seeking some clarity before exploring some of the more 'eco-friendly' perceptions which are described in the following chapter.

Understanding something of the selling of consumerism

Why did Charles Kettering CEO of General Motors once say *"The key to economic prosperity is the organised creation of dissatisfaction"*? This cartoon by Polyp suggests that consumerism is a kind of addiction.

Source: Polyp

Making it an addiction may have had something to do with the work of this man, Edward Bernays.

Bernays invented public relations in the 1920s. He was also Freud's nephew and really understood how to use his uncle's insight into human nature. Freud believed that:

Source: Photo by Nickolas Muray, copyright Nickolas Muray Photo Archives. Courtesy of George Eastman House

66 Man, far from being in charge of his faculties, is controlled by darkly primitive forces, libidinous and savage desires that lead to war. 99

As a corporate public relations man, Bernays had a more positive spin on the general theory. This is explained by journalist Andrew Billen.

66 Yes, the unconscious could lead man to war, but it could also lead him to the department store. And if his motives were invisible to himself, they need not be to his masters, who could manipulate them, whipping them, for instance, into fits of hatred against the Other or into a lust for possessions they did not need. 99

USA corporations needed Bernays because they became worried, around the mid 20th century that demand for products might dry up as consumers met their needs. Production was becoming so large scale and its products relatively cheap that consumers were saving more, not spending. The answer was to sell products by appealing to the irrational, emotional side of human life, to sell 'lifestyle' and aspiration. In short, Bernays said that selling products as substitutes for emotional needs created an endless market, for products could never actually satisfy emotional needs.

🌍 Breaking taboos

In the 1920s Edward Bernays was paid by the USA Tobacco Foundation to find a way of breaking the taboo against women smoking in public. He realised that cigarettes were a symbol of male power and thus the subject of women's envy; so he announced that cigarettes were 'torches of freedom' and that women's liberation lay in lighting up. Well dressed young actresses were employed to join street marches about women's equality and to smoke cigarettes, especially if newsreel cameras were around. It worked well. But, of course, nicotine addiction didn't actually make women freer – cigarettes just made them feel freer.

Understanding consumerism in this way is a changed perception every bit as much as recognising the economy as a 'waste economy.'

❝ *We have become slaves of our own desires, and we have forgotten we can become more than that.* **❞**

Adam Curtis, producer of *The Century of Self*, BBC

Hence the classic confusion, deliberately introduced, of More with Better. After all, 'more' is a quantitative term and 'better' is qualitative. 'Better' is better! As the writer Daniel Boorstin noted: *"If you link products, narratives and personalities to emotional desires and feelings, they become powerful emotional symbols"*. Consumerism and religion rely on this; Joseph Goebells used the same methods to further the plans of his Führer.

If you appeal to the imagination rather than rational thinking, you gain power. Napoleon knew this, and once said that *"imagination rules the world"*. Educating for some sort of sustainable world will have to engage learners with the very same irrational forces, with imagination, 'lifestyles' and the emotions. It is almost inevitable that it will have to suggest a more satisfactory world-view, something learners can believe is a more accurate description of how the world works.

The danger is in falling into ready-made solutions. There is a strong group of educators who understand the arguments in these chapters about unsustainable development: their roots go back at least as far as the Romantic movement and those poets, artists and writers who condemned the godless industrial revolution. But their modern day solutions are often – so far as they have filtered into mainstream schooling – still reminiscent of a pre-industrial mindset of spirit, social order, crafts and community.

For them it is a question of morals and ethics, of individuals and community making up their mind to act differently, whether this is in litter campaigns, riverside clean-ups, tree planting, or green and ethical consumerism. 'If only we all ...recycled ...walked to school ...took a basket to the shops ...grew our own vegetables ...respected each other ...grew spiritually.'

If only... and while there is much to be said for all of these things its just not a way forward for the majority. It's not a message which engages with the future constructively because it sounds like "*a lifelong celery diet*" as Paul Hawken so vividly put it. It sounds like less and less, a world of sacrifice and at its worst of 'one acre and a cow' peasantry.

But what were we dreaming of?

If looking back to some kind of low key existence is just not acceptable to the majority it is still important to be able to challenge the 'more = better' identity in a contemporary way.

It seems more doesn't equal happier – above a certain (moderate) level of consumption. It may be possible to discuss '*How much is enough?*' (see 2.3).

But still there is the sense that ESD is happier identifying problems and looking back than providing frameworks through which a sustainable world might be visible. In short, we know what we are against but not what we are for. The next chapter explores new metaphors and world-views for clues to the future.

(i) 2.3

Happiness is limited
(that's lucky as the planet is too)

Here's a shocking fact. Despite a huge increase in wealth, people in Europe and the more developed nations have grown no happier in the past 50 years. This should encourage a major rethink – from attitudes to consumerism, the balance between life and work, to priorities for health and even moral philosophy.

If people are asked how happy they are, their replies indicate no increase in happiness. This is true of Britain, the US, Europe and Japan. Even in the so-called golden age up to the 1970s, there was no increase. And, except in Japan, there were well-documented increases in depression, alcoholism and crime. Modern neuroscience confirms that what people say about their happiness does indeed correspond to an objective reality about which we now have an increasing amount of hard knowledge.

The picture is different in poor countries where happiness has risen when people have got richer. If you are near the bread line, absolute income is a matter of life and death. But things are different in the 'more developed world'. Since the Second World War people have become richer. They travel more; they live longer, and they are healthier. But they are no happier.

Why has extra income brought so little extra happiness? There are two main reasons. The first is rivalry, or keeping up with the Joneses. We compare our income and living standards with others. If others live better, we feel worse off unless we too live better. And there is also habituation. We compare what we have with what we are used to. If I live better today, I shall feel worse next year unless I keep up with this year's standard. So I am on a kind of treadmill where, each time I improve myself, I set myself a higher hurdle for the future.

In both these ways our efforts to become better off are in part self-defeating. For if I move up relative to you, you move back relative to me. My extra income is polluting your experience. Similarly, if I move up my own standards today, I raise my own standards for tomorrow. Unless I foresee this, it is a form of self-pollution – an addiction, like smoking...

Source: Adapted from *Don't worry, be happy (and pay your taxes)*. It is based on the work of Richard Layard, co-director of the London School of Economics Centre for Economic Performance. His three Robbins lectures on happiness are on http://cep.lse.ac.uk

Chapter 3
State of mind II

" *If we don't change where we're going, we may get there. If we want to go somewhere else, we need stars to steer by. Perhaps the first step is to describe the sort of destination we want to reach.* **"**

Amory Lovins (1999) *Natural Capitalism Ch 13*

" *The major problems in the world are the result of the difference between the way nature works and the way man thinks.* **"**

Gregory Bateson, ecologist

Ideas are what we steer by. Behind ideas are metaphors, such as the notion that the world is machine-like; a world of parts, of cause and effect and in principle predictable. Seeing the world as a machine or *mechanistically and fragmentarily* is not a purchase on some fundamental truth but just a metaphor to help humans grasp some scientific abstractions. It works well enough within certain limits – missiles fly, arrows fall, engines run, society and economies seem manageable; knowledge is arbitrarily divided up and students are thereby instructed... But the real world now looks more complicated and uncertain.

The emerging world-view is that humans are *participants* in a complex *system* comprised of the earth and its biosphere.

Ecology has an important role in reminding humankind about the interconnectedness of life and the physical and biological systems which make up the 'ecosphere' and by pointing out the increasingly obvious limits to the ecosphere's ability to absorb wastes and provide resources. In physics, by the early 20th century Newton's world was seen to be only a part of the picture, the so called Laws of Nature only operated between certain limits. In the very big, cosmic scale and in the very small, sub-atomic scale they fell away. Uncertainty entered the world and it has never left.

The advent of computing allowed mathematicians to model dynamic (moving) systems and here they found the world is turbulent, stable within certain parameters for sure but flowing unevenly. They found that large-scale change can be brought about by very small events amplified within a system – and in a very short time. The mathematics of a *non linear* world also showed that change could arise anywhere, and that whole systems shaped the operation of their sub wholes, parts were no longer the simple fundamentals of how the world operated: everything was contextualised. Everything mattered. In subjects as far apart as physics and economics, education and climatology insights about a more dynamic flowing interconnected and uncertain world shaped themselves around metaphors which were often 'organic' or 'holographic' because a machine metaphor no longer fitted.

Perhaps the single most important icon of a changed perspective is that of the image of the Earth from the moon, it is used almost universally by environmental organisations and it displays the Earth as one jewel-like living entity in dark space. It also shows the system as a whole – One Earth.

Symbolically the straight line, linear world of Progress was replaced by the circle, a 'magical' often religious symbol of the world's interconnectedness. In ancient times identified with *ourouboros* the snake eating its tail: a symbol of death and regeneration: of sustainability.

3.1

Ouroboros – a symbol of death and regeneration: of sustainability

(i) 3.1
'So what?' Do world-views matter?

Yes. According to scientist and philosopher David Bohm we do not choose our intentions. How we act depends on what sense we make of the world and this sense is essentially metaphorical. More than this, we operate habitually, we tend to react to new situations using old patterns – hence the comment that the hardest thing to change in life is one's own mind .

If we participate in the ecosphere and see it as an interconnected flowing whole then it follows that humans don't control and *cannot* control these dynamic and turbulent systems however much they try (because all the variables are not known and minute changes can be amplified through the system rapidly). If not control then humans can *influence* and must do so with care. Many things then follow, for example, adopting the *precautionary principle* is obvious – putting the onus on those proposing to introduce change to show that it's safe. 'Working with nature not against it', becomes more than a cliche and almost an axiom. The idea of 'zero emissions' becomes an unexceptional rather than absurd target...

An educationalist looks at contrasting world-views

More than a decade ago, Sue Greig, David Selby and Greg Pike, influenced explicitly by David Bohm, discussed how world-views panned out in education in their seminal book *Greenprints*. They included a version of this table:

world-view	theory of change	curriculum and instruction position
fragmentalism humankind is divorced from nature and can therefore exploit the environment; nature is made up of a series of building blocks; individuals are encouraged to compete in the market place as free agents	**traditional/conservative** traditions must be maintained – change needs to be checked and controlled; parts of a system can be changed if they do not work effectively; social change comes about through the efforts of successful individuals	**transmission** education is a one-way top downward movement of certain knowledge, skills and values; its focus is the traditional school subjects taught in a traditional way; the student is seen as a passive recipient of convenienty packaged and programmed blocks of teaching
pragmatism (modern scientific) humankind can improve the environment through the use of rational planning; science and techology can solve the problems the planet faces; individual behaviour is predictable and can be monitored through legislation	**intervention** change needs to be introduced and managed in a rational and scientific manner; social improvement requires deliberate intervention by some individuals for the good of others	**transaction** education is a dialogue between the student and the curriculum; the focus is on teaching strategies which facilitate problem solving; the student is seen as rational and capable of solving problems if given the right tools
holism (systems-thinking) all life on the planet is interconnected and interdependent; meaning is derived from understanding relationships; individuals cannot act in isolation – the actions of any one impact on the system	**organicism** change is an inevitable and natural function of a system; change only has meaning in the context of the system; social improvement comes through dismantling the human-made barriers to change	**transformation** education is a process of personal and social development; it focusses on the aesthetic, moral, physical and spiritual needs of the student as well as her cognitive attainment; the student is viewed as a whole person

John Miller in *Greenprints for Changing Schools*, Greig, Selby and Pike (1989) p45

Once more it is evident that the world-view shapes what is observed in other, perhaps all contexts. In an aspiring 'education for sustainability', as in education generally, we are perhaps somewhere between 'transmission' and 'transaction' with aspirations to 'transformation'?

And in economics here is a model of a 'natural' economy modeled on a living system with an emphasis on feedback loops. Providing the sun still shines – it is based on solar energy – it is arguably a fuller description or model of an economy which could be sustainable as opposed to the earlier, linear model (p. 26). It is quite simply *consistent with the systemic metaphors we have been exploring* and derives some of its power to explain and influence from that source.

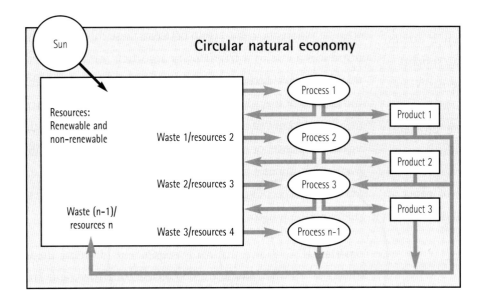

FSC

With the insight gained from the discussion on world-views its clear that there is literally no *context* for this representation. It all floats in an unconstrained space. The economy can grow and grow without limit and the economy is somehow largely separate from the other factors which are, in turn, separate from each other. Sustainable development is a sort of choice about integrating something of each.

This is exactly in line with the old fragmentary and mechanistic viewpoint: business as usual (more = better) but now 'greener and fairer' (economic growth provides the means to protect the environment, make production cleaner and promote 'social progress') It implies some reform but humankind still does largely what it pleases (world without limit). For many people this is OK, but by applying a different perspective or 'world-view' the diagram looks like this...

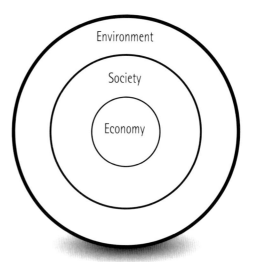

The ecosphere ('environment') is the context within which everything takes place. It has limits – of which we are becoming gradually aware – and these cannot be broken without risking catastrophe (a loss of life support). As it is a complex interconnected world, physical systems providing environmental services and of course biodiversity are protected; since we participate in the web of life. Next comes a society with an improving *quality* of life – since it cannot be a society of more and more it will be a society of better and better – and fairer. To provide for that development, within the limits of the ecosphere is the economy – with the economy as a means of servicing human needs rather than people and resources servicing the economy. This would mean redesigning almost every aspect of human life, such is the upside down nature of the current situation where economy is dominant.

So is sustainability 'business as usual but greener and fairer' or does it mean 'redesign everything!' 'Material Progress' or 'Enriched Sufficiency'? Or is it somewhere in between...?

66 If systems theory has taught us anything, it is that systems are complexly interconnected, in which a system influences and is influenced by another system. The individual who wishes to change the world has little direct influence on governmental policies and global interactions, but the individual does influence a family, and a family influences a community, and a community influences a city, and a city influences a state, and a state influences a nation, and before you know it the whole world is changed because of a few individuals who give a damn. 99

Dave Allen et al, Trinity University in San Antonio, Texas
http://www.resnet.trinity.edu/ebakhtia/sustainability/conclusion.html

New knowledge for new worlds?

It is worth quoting Napoleon again: "imagination rules the world". Luckily thinkers and practical people alike are coming through with proposals which engage the imagination based on many of the insights of systems-thinking. These include writers and researchers, architects and business leaders such as Amory Lovins, Paul Hawken, Edwin Datschefski, Lester Brown, James Robertson and William McDonough to name a few. They are saying that there is much to look forward to, many ideas, technologies and systemic changes which can lead to at least a substantially more sustainable world – and provide a breathing space to allow us to tackle the deeper issues of poverty and inequality.

Educators need access to this new knowledge, especially about design and technology, about systems, about economics and how one flows into another. They also need to know more about motivation and behaviour, about how one gets from here to sustainability, the role of prices, the tax and spending of governments.

After all, for sustainable development to mean much to the majority a sparkling sense of what benefits it can bring is needed. The UN agrees (see Marketing 'Cool' Life-Styles p. 2). It has to become something to engage the emotions and the imagination. Put simply it has to be better than what exists now. ESD, intelligently, must always be as much about the possibilities of the future as the issues of the present. Lastly, it must help learners answer the question: What's In It For Me? (WIFM?)

Educators have to appreciate this, unequivocally, to be able to engage learners in the world of the possible future, a sustainable future. However, many shy away from the 'WIFM thinking' instinctively – it seems very base and almost primitive to do deals about something so obviously important as the state of the planet. Instead, like the optimistic Trinity University team quoted on this page, they feel that it can be done for altruistic reasons largely by a change of heart. It seems not (see 3.2).

Here are some starters on the 'new knowledge', some bald statements, plus some tasters in the form of further reading, any of which could make a useful discussion in a workshop context.

- *We are inevitably moving from oil and nuclear towards a solar/hydrogen economy. A clean energy economy*

- *Business: the best way to deal with waste is to design it out not to collect it up. Waste = food. Production is 'cradle to cradle' (see p.44)*

- *We don't want consumer durables per se but the services they provide – I don't want a fridge, just chilled or frozen food*

- *Prices are messages. They must tell the truth about social and environmental costs and this includes taxes and subsidies. p.s. Tax materials, energy and waste not people.*

> **❝** *The older, wiser environmental movement understands…that the planet cannot be saved by a voluntary change of lifestyle on the part of individuals, but only through collective action – changing laws and economic rules to change people's perception of their short-term self-interest.* **❞**

Editorial: The Independent
http://news.independent.co.uk/world/environment/

ⓘ 3.2

Further information

A look at the Community Based Social Marketing website and associated research makes clear that education alone is not sufficient to change behaviour even when the principle of what is being taught is accepted http://www.cbsm.com

This insight also tends to undermine many naive views of motivating and sustaining student action on behalf of the environment.

For a thorough briefing one book above all makes the case for being optimistic *Natural Capitalism* by Amory Lovins *et al* (1999) much of which can be read online at http://www.natcap.org

Have a look at who is quoted in this item…

> *I believe fuel cell vehicles will finally end the hundred-year reign of the internal combustion engine as the dominant source of power for personal transportation. It's going to be a winning situation all the way around — consumers will get an efficient power source, communities will get zero emissions, and automakers will get another major business opportunity — a growth opportunity.*

William C. Ford, Jr.

 Yes, that's just one of four heads of large motor or oil companies to come out and declare for hydrogen fuel cells.
3.3

> *All roads in the clean energy industry lead to a hydrogen economy in which we can use renewable energy to make hydrogen, and use hydrogen to power our cars, homes, and factories. The big question is how do we get there?*

Joel Makower, founder of CleanEdge.com, which tracks the progress of the clean technology market.

ⓘ 3.3

A fuel cell? A scientific briefing

In principle, a fuel cell operates like a battery. Unlike a battery, a fuel cell does not run down or require recharging. It will produce energy in the form of electricity and heat as long as fuel is supplied.

A fuel cell consists of two electrodes sandwiched around an electrolyte. Oxygen passes over one electrode and hydrogen over the other, generating electricity, water and heat.

Hydrogen fuel is fed into the anode of the fuel cell. Oxygen (or air) enters the fuel cell through the cathode. Encouraged by a catalyst, the hydrogen atom splits into a proton and an electron, which take different paths to the cathode. The proton passes through the electrolyte. The electrons create a separate current that can be utilized before they return to the cathode, to be reunited with the hydrogen and oxygen in a molecule of water.

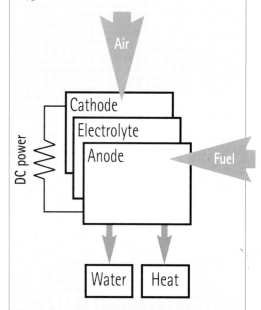

Ideally hydrogen will be supplied by electrolysis using renewable energies. A fuel cell system which includes a 'fuel reformer' can utilize the hydrogen from any hydrocarbon fuel – from natural gas to methanol, and even gasoline. Since the fuel cell relies on chemistry and not combustion, emissions from this type of a system would still be much smaller than emissions from the cleanest fuel combustion processes.

Source: Fuel Cells 2000 www.fuelcells.org

Examples of changed perspectives

Here are some concrete examples of change arranged as brief 'stimulus resources' for discussion. A reference is supplied for in-depth work.

🌍 I want a washing machine. Why? I want clean clothes.

Beginning in the mid-1980s, Swiss industry analyst Walter Stahel and German chemist Michael Braungart independently proposed a new industrial model that is now gradually taking shape. Rather than an economy in which goods are made and sold, these visionaries imagined a service economy wherein consumers obtain services by leasing or renting goods rather than buying them outright. (Their plan should not be confused with the conventional definition of a service economy, in which burger-flippers outnumber steelworkers.) Manufacturers cease thinking of themselves as sellers of products and become, instead, deliverers of service, provided by long-lasting, upgradeable durables. Their goal is selling results rather than equipment, performance and satisfaction rather than motors, fans, plastics, or condensers.

The system can be demonstrated by a familiar example. Instead of purchasing a washing machine, consumers could pay a monthly fee to obtain the service of having their clothes cleaned. The washer would have a counter on it, just like an office photocopier, and would be maintained by the manufacturer on a regular basis, much the way mainframe computers are. If the machine ceased to provide its specific service, the manufacturer would be responsible for replacing or repairing it at no charge to the customer, because the washing machine would remain the property of the manufacturer. The concept could likewise be applied to computers, cars, DVD players, video decks, refrigerators, and almost every other durable that people now buy, use up, and ultimately throw away. Because products would be returned to the manufacturer for continuous repair, reuse, and remanufacturing, Stahel called the process 'cradle-to-cradle'.

Source: see
http://www.natcap.org/sitepages/art78.php

Reduce emissions and boost profits?

It's not 'profits or poisons'. More often than not it is in a business's interest to reduce waste.

 L'Oreal

'It may sound dubious, but take the example of L'Oreal, the world's largest cosmetics manufacturer. Between 1990 and 2000, the company increased production by 60% but decreased greenhouse emissions by 44%. L'Oreal Engineering Director Ken Kraly attributes those results in large part to 'value-added' energy conservation programs. A high-efficiency lighting installation in one L'Oreal facility, for example, cost $180,000; the resulting electricity savings in the first year were $160,000 – nearly a one-year payback, and equivalent savings were generated every year thereafter. In addition to re-gasketing airdampers, tightening steam traps, insulating boilers, and other such negligibly sexy conservation measures, Kraly implemented a large-scale recycling program to reduce waste incineration from 1,000 tons per year in 1990 to under 300 tons in 2000 (despite the spike in production levels). The result was a $500,000 savings in waste removal costs and a whopping 72% reduction of greenhouse gas emissions related to incineration.'

Amanda Griscom

Source: 'In good company' http://www.alternet.org/

 66 *The essential need is to develop highly self-sufficient, small-scale socio-economic systems, so that people in a suburb or town can provide for themselves most of the goods and services they need... these conserver ways would not involve hardship or deprivation and would actually provide a higher quality of life than we have now.* **99**

Ted Trainer

3.4

 3.4

Sustainable Products

There are five design requirements for sustainable products. The first three mimic the way plant and animal ecosystems work:

Cyclic: The product is made from organic materials, and is recyclable or compostable, or is made from minerals that are continuously cycled in a closed loop.

Solar: The product uses solar energy or other forms of renewable energy that are cyclic and safe, both during use and manufacture.

Safe: The product is non-toxic in use and disposal, and its manufacture does not involve toxic releases or the disruption of ecosystems.

The fourth requirement is based on the need to maximise the utility of resources in a finite world:

Efficient: The product's efficiency in manufacture and use is improved by a factor of ten, requiring 90% less materials, energy and water than products providing equivalent utility did in 1990.

And the fifth recognises that all companies have an impact on the people who work for them and the communities within which they operate:

Social: The product and its components and raw materials are manufactured under fair and just operating conditions for the workers involved and the local communities.

Source: http://www.biothinking.com

▼ Workshop activity idea

How many products are produced in this way?

How could this be encouraged – if you agree with the proposal?

Source: http://www1.tpgi.com.au/

Rejecting consumer cultural values?

There is still the hearts and minds battle set within all these practical suggestions and technological predictions. Consumerism is a key challenge and here too more sophisticated approaches to upsetting advertising and consumer culture have emerged. Since advertising has become so visual it is not surprising to see examples of satire in a visual format.

See http://www.adbusters.org for examples and discussion.

At the other end of the spectrum are the arguments about economics and prices. The very first paragraph of (i) 3.5 belongs on any ESD course*. A lesson on prices is a kind of touchstone as to how realistic the course is. After all *Prices… largely determine decisions by producers and consumers… there is a direct causal connection between mispricing and unsustainable development.*

End of the beginning

Looking forward to a sustainable future means being informed and enthusiastic about what is possible as well as recognising and criticising unsustainable practices and vested interests. There is no doubt that resource efficiency can be increased between 10 and 100 times, that energy can be clean and safe, that houses can be warm (or cool) and comfortable and cheap to keep that way; that employment can be creative and interesting, that poverty can be drastically reduced, democracy can be renewed and a local economy can meet many of our needs. *Imagining* life under those circumstances is a first step, especially for educators and learners whose primary domain is the development of the person, mind, body and spirit. A second is in exploring the route to that future with openness, since what might look like part of a solution now could still turn out to be a part of the problem – look at the idea of the paperless office!

---

* Significantly, very few existing ESD courses pre-16 engage with prices and markets other than introducing misinformation such as 'a green product costs more', without considering what it means by 'cost'.

Chapter 4
Learning how to learn – sustainability

66 *Optimism is a strategy for making a better future. Because unless you believe that the future can be better, it's unlikely you will step up and take responsibility for making it so.* **99**

Noam Chomsky

Taking stock. Over the last few decades the changes described in Chapter 1 brought the world, or at least some of it to the conclusion that a form of 'balanced development' was needed. Called 'sustainable development', it had multiple interpretations, not least as the term translated with different nuances across the peoples of the world. In Russia it has suggested 'steadiness' whereas in Hungary it is equated with 'good governance'. In some studies, over 300 definitions of sustainable development have been identified. It is hardly surprising that education too adopted a multitude of interpretations. This frustrates some educators, who feel they need to know the boundaries of things, to know how one thing is different from another if they are to teach it well. Schools often adopt this view and the already crowded curriculum gets ever more crowded, since there is no end of knowledge and no end to the ways in which it can be parcelled up. The roots of this *fragmentary* world-view have been described in Chapter 2.

A more satisfying way of looking at both sustainable development and education is to think in terms of process and context. This might well be consistent with emerging world-views which are more *dynamic* and *systemic* (process and context!) To help create a sense of process or movement the term *sustainability* rather than sustainable development is often used.

FSC

> **66** Sustainability is not a concept referring to some static paradise, but rather a capacity of human beings to continuously adapt to their non-human environments by means of social organisation. **99**
>
> Prof Wm Scott

Source: Scott (2002) *Sustainability and Learning*

After all, dynamic world-views stress 'feedback', 'connectedness' and movement as primary features and therefore sustainability cannot be 'another thing' anymore than history or geography is a discrete entity. They are useful categories and abstractions. Perhaps, as Prof Scott points out, sustainability can be seen "*as a process through which we shall need to learn to live more in tune with the environment. But, it is not enough to say that sustainable development and learning need to go hand-in-hand. Rather, it is crucial to recognise that sustainable development will not be taking place where learning is not happening. To put this another way: sustainable development is a learning process through which we can (if we choose) learn to build our capacity to live more sustainably.*

There is little emphasis here on teaching. This is for two reasons: the first is that much of the learning we shall need to do will be beyond the school, college, and university system; it will be learning in, between and by institutions, organisations and communities — where most of our learning goes on anyway.

The second is that as we don't yet know what exactly we shall need to learn in relation to sustainable development, it's hard to know in detail what needs to be taught — except, perhaps, how to learn."

And here is the crucial point, put another way.

Here are the problems – wow they are huge, reach everywhere and to every level, and they are all connected! It looks like big waves breaking...

Source: www.istockphoto.com

'Learning more than teaching', 'systemic metaphors', 'sustainability' … It all appears to be a long way from the concerns and enthusiasms of many committed environmentalists and environmental educators. For them, engaging the emotions of young people, promoting the understanding and protection of Nature, while marvelling at its innate beauty still seem to be core activities. A short excursion through history might help explain why.

Going back to go forward

The Wildwood – a primitive and potentially hostile place

The Romantic movement was a reaction to the industrialisation of the UK, mainland Europe and the USA. It articulated the feelings of many that this progress of science and technology, this engineering of the natural world and humankind was soulless and one-sided. It was damaging to local culture and craftsmanship and was a wicked despoilation of Nature. 'Nature' should also be recognised, celebrated and preserved – it had, until the 18th century, been perceived as either wasteland or a hostile environment. So as industry spread, that sense that wild places should be protected grew, not least for the necessary recreation, education and indeed health of the growing urban masses worldwide. A strand of this eventually entered schools under what was called 'Nature Studies'.

As the various strands of nature studies evolved it became more science based: environmental education had its roots in an appreciation of wild places but it became informed by botany, biology and ecology – that study of interconnectedness everyone understands as 'the web of life' – and our part in it. In many ways this is what schools still understand, deep down. It has always been a mix of 'love' and 'see, understand and do'. The story goes like this: nature is wonderful. It deserves and can benefit from our protection. 'The world is in our hands' is an over-used illustration found on posters, book covers, 'green' magazines and world conferences but it has very deep resonances.

The world in our hands – a recurring theme

Environmental education became a curious mix: emotional response tempered by scientific understanding and a belief in reason as the sure judge and guide to sound policy and good citizenship. As a result, schools promoted 'caring for nature' in a variety of ways. These included creating and maintaining wildlife habitats – from bird boxes to gardens or simple wild areas – nature observation, encouraging attendance at summer camps, or field centres, measuring changes in the local environment and gaining knowledge, largely scientific, about plants and animals, about physical processes and some of the chemistry and biology behind words like 'pollution.'

'Environmental Action' was considered important in many schools, almost as an indicator of the urgency of concerns about the environment – that 'just do it' feeling encountered right at the start of Chapter 1. Eventually this included looking very close to home: reducing litter, planting trees and saving water or energy in schools at the level of closing off leaking taps and switching off lights. Many teachers worked in this practical environmental education with little more than their enthusiasm and commitment to keep them going. They still do.

All of this is necessary, and rewarding, but, sadly, it is no longer sufficient. Perhaps it never was, but now we have the benefit of hindsight.

Inevitably, ideas and practice have moved along. Some teachers will say: *"Well, we have a broad environmental education now you know. In the sciences and geography particularily, students learn of pollution, the greenhouse effect; the fate of people and places; of development and change from agriculture to industry and beyond that to services and the information age."*

Agreed. Looking at the bigger picture, however, pan-European research suggests that much of what teachers call 'environmental education' is weak on those two other partners of sustainability – the social and the economic. Here is an extract from the University of Muenster's research:

 Conceptually (lessons) are characterized by the individualizing and moralizing of environmental problems. Aspects of economics and social sciences which are essential to the development and solution of environmental problems as well as the importance of structures which stimulate environmentally more compatible behaviour have not been considered enough in environmental education yet. **"**

> ### ⓘ 4.1
> **The world awakes**
>
> 1972   First World Summit on Environment, Stockholm
>
> 1989   Brundtland commission first mentions 'sustainable development'
>
> 1992   Rio Conference on Environment and Development introduces SD onto world stage
>
> 2002   World Summit on Sustainable Development, Johannesburg
>
> 2005   UN Decade of Education for Sustainable Development begins

Source: University of Muenster

66 Sustainable development – a dynamic process that enables all people to realise their potential and to improve their quality of life in ways which simultaneously protect and enhance the Earth's life support systems. 99

Forum for the Future

66 ...environmental education tends to neglect the socio-economic and cultural dimensions of environmental problems or rather deals with them in an inadequately reduced way. 99

Environmental education in practice is partial. Even 'environmental education' as a name does not adequately reflect all three dynamics of sustainable development – ecology (environment) society and economy. The definition (left) illustrates a more sophisticated approach.

In education for sustainable development or learning for sustainability such a 'dynamic process' might mean learning styles that are iterative ('feeds into itself' – see Chapter 5). It is inclusive ('enables all people' – has a social justice strand) and it is not about how much material wealth we have so much as the 'quality of life' (and discerning the difference... what an important discussion that is!) and, yes, 'protect' but also 'enhance Earth's life support systems'.

Note the implied futures dimension, a sense of possibility. No wonder the phrase 'environmental education' or its socially focussed sister 'development education' or 'global education' does not usually capture what is meant by the full flowering of an education for sustainability.

And apart from the niceties of language another problem for teachers using a conventional approach is that learners become ever more cynical as they get older: about what they have been told and what they have done. They only had to look around them. Students could see that the business of the school was firstly, grades and certification, that environmental knowledge or skills, while it had a place, was a marginal concern; that the very operation of the school itself, its use of energy and water, its handling of waste and the management of the building was very wasteful of resources and that there was little sustained commitment to change. And while fair trade coffee might have made an inroad into the staffroom or office it was far from being part of an 'ethical procurement strategy'. For streetwise youngsters being told one message while all around other values and prorities are revealed is deeply instructive. Like Father Christmas, environmental education became something only little kids believed in.

In some schools and colleges environmental education looked like a kind of religious education – it was a personal calling, a moral and ethical position based on the individual's commitment, and instead of arguing about the number of angels that could fit onto the head of a pin the discussion was 'paper or plastic for cups?'.

It became a very powerful strand of thinking: "*Like religious teaching, sustainable development education has the potential to form and transform personal behaviour and the way society is organised*".

Source: Prof Shirley Ali Khan *Greening the FE Curriculum 2003*

Outside of the 'faith' a very secular world carried on much the same. Indeed, in a world of global brands and extensive product advertising, rapidly changing technologies and employment, the pressure to earn money, to be a good consumer and improve one's life eventually overwhelmed the typically naive, but environmentally and socially concerned young person. After all, what was the alternative? Youngsters wanted to know the way out of the crisis, but sometimes all they got was to hold hands in a circle. Schools simply did not explore *realistic* alternative futures and how to get there: in many ways the legacy of environmental education was not 'empowerment' at all, but guilt. And pessimism.

See the activity based on the *Prisoner's Dilemma* (p. 103) for help in understanding why, in most circumstances, personal commitment to the environment is simply irrational.

Re-orientation can be rewarding

Providing that educators *are* prepared to re-evaluate the balance of what they do and its impact with learners, an education for sustainability can surely encompass the good moral works of old, the useful environmental science and add to social awareness. It inevitably demands engagement in the 'bigger picture', the worlds of the consumer brands, consumer behaviour, international trade, government, business, social justice and technology, taxes and spending but most of all, with the possibilities of the future. In order to live in a sustainable world people have to be able to imagine it and how they might realistically get from here to there. As sustainability is forever and always a learning process educators need to hold up to scrutiny the best and the most promising of the ideas and visions about

4.1: Traffic

4.2: World registrations of vehicles over time

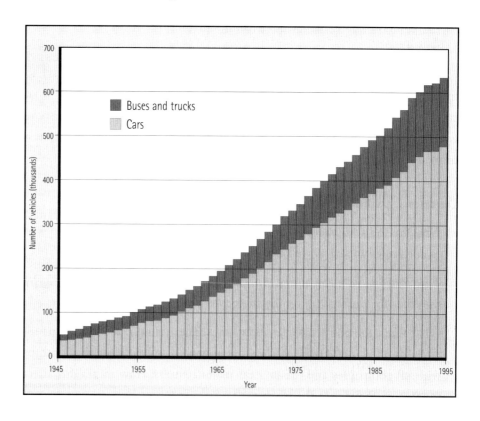

4.3: Changes in the real cost of transport and income

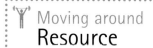
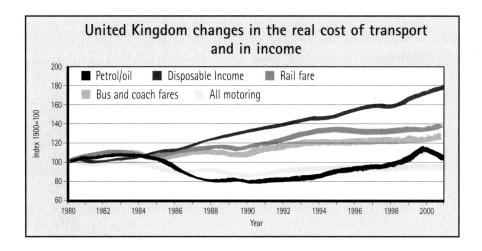

United Kingdom changes in the real cost of transport and in income

- Petrol/oil
- Disposable Income
- Rail fare
- Bus and coach fares
- All motoring

Source: DfT (UK) 2003

- The overall cost of motoring (including purchase, maintenance, petrol and oil, tax and insurance) has remained at or below its 1980 level in real terms, although the real cost of fuel is now 12% higher than in 1980, despite a fall in 2001.

- Public transport fares have risen in real terms over the last 20 years. In 2001, bus and coach fares were 31% higher and rail fares 37% higher than in 1980.

- Over the same period, average disposable income has gone up more than 80% in real terms. Transport has therefore become more affordable, with a greater improvement in the affordability of car use than that of public transport.

- The average number of trips made by car has increased by 24% since 1985/86, from 517 to 639. All of this increase occurred by 1995/97.

- Since 1985/86 there has been a continual decline in the number of trips made on foot, from 350 to 263. Trips by bicycle or motorcycle have also fallen by 44%, from 34 to 19.

- Trips made by rail or London Underground have increased slightly since 1995/97, from 18 to 20 trips a year. However, the number of trips made by local bus has fallen by 31% since 1985/86, from 83 to 57.

« The growth in car travel and fall in bus patronage seen over the last twenty years have been accompanied by stable motoring costs and rising bus fares. »

Source: Department for Transport *Transport Statistics, Transport Trends 2002* Jan 2003 Section Two

See: http://www.dft.gov.uk

 *4.4:* Subsidising big oil

There is growing awareness in the USA that the full cost of using oil for transportation is 'subsidized' – that is, petrol prices paid by consumers do not reflect the full economic cost to society. The true cost is hidden by many direct and indirect public subsidies, which include:

• reduced corporate income taxes for the oil industry (average 11% compared to 18% in other industries)

• lower than average sales taxes on gasoline (3% compared to 6% on other goods)

• government funding of programs that primarily benefit the oil industry and motorists

• 'hidden' environmental costs caused by motor vehicles, namely air, water, and noise pollution (estimated at between 52 and 185 billion dollars a year).

Source: *Union of Concerned Scientists in the USA*

For more detail see: 'Subsidizing big oil'
http://www.ucsusa.org/clean_vehicles/

Congestion charge cuts jams

Average traffic speeds have risen to 11mph. The congestion charge has cut traffic jams by 40% on London's roads, the first full review of the scheme has found.

Mayor Ken Livingstone predicted congestion would be cut by between 20% and 30%, which would have raised at least £130m towards London's public transport.

But the latest findings from Transport for London (TfL) show the £5 daily charge to drive into central London has reduced jams by nearly twice that amount.

Traffic speeds are up by one third, although the average speed is still only 11mph, meaning the average driver is spending 13% less time in his car.

Mr Livingstone said the results meant even the scheme's sceptics would have to recognise its benefits.

He added: "Fewer traffic jams and faster, more-reliable journey times into and within central London are good for business, tourism and Londoners."

But many businesses say they have been affected in some way by the charge, as fewer customers are prepared to drive in.

The report also found 2,000 motorists have switched to the Tube at rush hour and 6,000 are taking the bus.

An average of 98,000 motorists and 12,000 fleet vehicles pay the charge every day.

Source BBC

Links ... the London Congestion Charge home page: http://www.cclondon.com/

A protest page: http://www.sod-u-ken.co.uk/

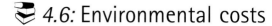
Oil and motor vehicle use are responsible for enormous hidden environmental costs. Economists term these costs 'externalities' because they are not included in the private costs of transportation. Nevertheless, these costs are real and they are borne by society at large. They include the money costs of air, water, and noise pollution. Reducing the costs of externalities requires government attention.

Transportation is responsible for most of the major air pollutants made in our urban areas, including particulate matter, carbon monoxide, and hydrocarbons and nitrogen oxides, which form ground-level ozone. In addition, motor vehicles are responsible for carcinogenic chemical emissions, carbon dioxide emissions (the principal greenhouse gas), water pollution (leaky underground storage tanks, oil spills, and road runoff), and noise. Pollution costs are borne by society in the form of increased health care costs and loss of wages due to illness and premature death (i.e. morbidity and mortality costs), reduced agricultural output, loss of visibility, and damage to buildings.

A 1995 study estimates the total cost in 1991 of environmental externalities to be $54 billion to $232 billion. Human deaths and illness due to air pollution account for over three-quarters of the total environmental cost and could be as high as $182 billion annually. For the Los Angeles area, it is estimated that the annual health-based cost from ozone and particulate exposure alone to be almost $10 billion.

Source: *Union of Concerned Scientists in the USA*
Adapted: http://www.ucsusa.org/clean_vehicles/

4.7: Aircar

After more than thirty years working with combustion engines, the French engineer Guy Negre has developed a concept of a totally non-polluting engine for use in urban areas.

This invention, which uses high pressure (300 bar) compressed air to store the energy needed for running the engine, is protected world-wide by more than 20 patents owned by the business he founded, MDI. In urban areas, the engine powers a five-seat vehicle with a range of approximately 200 km using 300 liters of compressed air (300 bar) stored in either carbon or glass fibre tanks. A compressor driven by an electric motor connected to a standard electric outlet does the 4 hour recharge of the compressed air tanks. A rapid recharge, using a high-pressure air pump, is also possible in around 3 minutes.

The car is cheap to produce and costs a few cents a kilometre to run. Negre claims it is also an excellent solution for African or other third world nations. Production is planned to begin in France and has several variants – a taxi, a pickup, a van and a sedan.

Source: MDI, France

Website: http://www.theaircar.com

Where does ESD belong?

Unsurprisingly, schools vary in how they want to include an education for sustainable development. In some countries it is mandated, in others there is only general guidance.

For the UK guidance and further links can be found at: **http://www.nc.uk.net/esd/gq1.htm**

Implementation ranges from separate courses under a heading like personal and social education; via integration into mainstream subject work, to add-on lessons in certain subjects, and special events such as the 'environment week' or an off-timetable day. Sometimes it is simply a reworking of programmes of study in certain subjects to reflect changing perceptions.

This book clearly isn't an off-the-shelf recipe book of ESD. There is plenty of conventional material around already, but in any case there is more at stake. It argues that unless the relationship between teacher and learner, or workshop leader and participant is productive, thoughtful, reflective and engaging then new and challenging ideas will be very difficult to work with satisfactorily – howsover they are organised. This is why there are classroom activities and workshop tasks at each stage of the book, each of which hopefully engages the practical professionalism of the teacher without prescribing a framework. With luck, the result is a skilled educator able to work confidently and creatively within the practical constraints and tensions of her own institution or circumstances. In short it takes an 'illuminative' approach based on supporting professional development (see also Chapter 6 and 7).

However, teachers often ask for general guidelines about changing the emphasis of their work or to identify some starting priorities. Here is one attempt at such a guideline ((i) 4.3 – and also *Briefing* Chapter 6). It makes the assumption that the teaching and learning is 'active' or dynamic and so it is worded as a series of questions or prompts for educators. Another assumption is that time in schools for ESD is limited and that *the most important questions should be paid most attention* (this also reflects diagram on p. 40 on how Environment, Society and Economics might relate in a sustainable world).

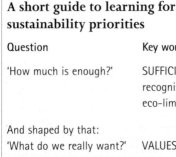

(i) 4.3

A short guide to learning for sustainability priorities

Question	Key words and Ideas
'How much is enough?'	SUFFICIENCY recognising eco-limits
And shaped by that: 'What do we really want?'	VALUES
...only then followed by: 'How can we provide ourselves with accessible goods and services at lowest overall resource cost?'	EFFICIENCY and EQUITY
'What should we do about waste?'	CLEANLINESS

Source Ken Webster, based on the work of Wolfgang Sachs and Alain Durning.

(i)
4.3

It is interestingly the *exact reverse* of most current school priorities in environmental education or sustainability work. Schools look at waste (from the production of energy, materials, and services and what to do about it, while leaving largely unquestioned possible limits to production (how much is enough?) and values (is 'more always better?' or is 'economic growth always a good thing?' and what is a 'good quality of life?') They have little to say on how eco-efficiency/eco-design can be encouraged (or even what it is) but are better on social justice (how is the benefit of production distributed?).

Logically, what to do about waste is not a big question if the other issues have been addressed – there simply won't be much waste! These rather obvious points do, sadly, emphasise how back-to-front much of our educational work can be.

Working through the examples (on ☰ 4.8) should help tease out the differences between more conventional approaches to the chosen themes of waste, energy and transport and the outlines of an education for sustainability. It is not possible to make any firm rules or define the boundary conditions as one is evolved from the other but as Prof Scott noted it has a lot to do with 'learning how to learn'. The next chapter has more to say on learning. Meanwhile this revision of a heading on a classroom blackboard seems to catch the moment for one young educator.

~~Why recycling is a good idea~~   Is recycling a good idea?

4.8: Example of revised planning for work on electricity and the social and environmental consequences of its production

Energy / Electricity

Common approach

a. assumes demand is rising and will always continue to rise. Assumes centralised production.
Impact on pollution locally and/or 'greenhouse effect' described

b. discusses different kinds of energy **supply** options – (nuclear, wind power, coal, gas, hydro, etc)

c. discussion of what we, the users of electricity could do to reduce demand. Domestic/school audit of electricity use.

d. students choose least polluting supply option and think about conservation of domestic/school electricity use?

ESD possibilities

a. why assume demand will always rise and why a centralised supply anyway? Investigate 'distributed generation'.

b. discussion of effectiveness of energy conservation vs new supply. It is better $ for $ invested

c. role of **prices** in electricity use. Can it be 'too cheap?' Problem of energy poverty. Incentives for reduced use?

d. students analyse industrial model of electricity supply and subsidies; discuss mix of investment in conservation, local generation and incentives to increase resource efficiency?

Notes:

Although these notes are aimed at educators – the language is adult and in a shorthand – it is clear that a very different lesson emerges, based on rather different assumptions. In the first the variables are different **supply options** and a call to **individual's altruistic behaviour**. In the second, basic assumptions are questioned, conservation and real cost pricing (**demand management**) get the place they deserve (scientifically) and the appeal is to individual or group interest via **incentives**. It is arguably more positive and futures-orientated.

In the jargon: accurate prices reflect real environmental and social costs and encourage technical innovation and efficiency.

'Y' Discuss this statement

The traditional lesson is 'business as usual but (a little) greener' and the second is locally focussed, incentivised, creative, sustainability-orientated. In fact, the context of the original lesson isn't about sustainability at all, for even if, in real life, more of the less polluting supply options ARE selected (not the cheapest?) its assumptions about how individuals behave is contradictory – we are supposed to be able to reduce demand by acting with conservation in mind yet overall demand is assumed to continue rising. It is simply not adequate for an education for sustainability.

Workshop tasks

Do you agree with this statement (see left)?

What about the syllabus – it is described mostly in terms of supply options!?

What about the novel supply technologies – hydrogen fuel cells etc?

'Y' A low energy future?

The house that Tony built (on his own, mostly). The local planning authority refused it permission to remain despite it having low impact.

Source: www.thatroundhouse.com

Workshop tasks

Is this what we think about when it comes to images of eco-living?

'Y' EE to ESD changing perspectives on recycling in schools

Everyone knows about recycling. Here is the symbol, the symbol so often indicative of sustainability – the circle plus the arrow heads to show movement and change.

Education tends to operate fragmentarily and when one sees work on 'recycling in action' this becomes very evident. For the most part it concerns itself with only one segment of that circle: that bit between shop, home and garbage bin and collection. For some strange reason this becomes 'recycling' to all intents and purposes.

It is a strange creature for another reason. The emphasis is very often on collecting and sorting waste – despite years of the reduce, reuse, recycle slogan – and once collected and shipped out of school what happens next is of lesser concern. What happens next is that the material goes to recycling firms who suffer from low but always fluctuating prices for the materials they collect. The commercial market for recycled materials is often very weak as a result. The very schools and youth groups who collect materials will often find their labours wasted: when the market fails the material is sent to incineration or landfill. In the worst cases it isn't even collected at all.

These same schools often do not purchase products made from recycled materials. From the fuss which is made one could expect every school to be stuffed with recycled paper, pens made from recycled traffic cones and rulers from old drinks cups. But no. Just tokenism most of the time. The educational messages of such an approach are horrendous but clear. If you only look at a part of the problem without understanding you will still be commended for your public spiritedness! Don't worry, nothing will really change.' It's a version of spin doctoring: all show and fine sentiments but insignificant results. You know where they learnt it!

Source: Ken Webster, reprinted from WWFlearning,
WWF UK's online educational resource 2002
www.wwflearning.co.uk

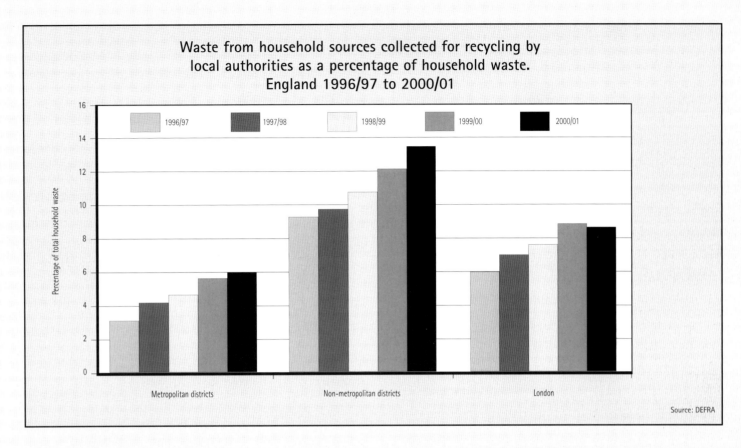

Waste from household sources collected for recycling by local authorities as a percentage of household waste. England 1996/97 to 2000/01

Source: DEFRA

Meaningful sustainability discussion is almost always achieved by searching out bigger perspectives first and the details second. This finding, or at least the search for the 'bigger picture' could be a key educational change in this area. In terms of priorities, don't worry about the actions 'to save the planet', schools are about *learning*. In the bigger picture the whole cycle is seen – and questions like this follow: Who has the most responsibility for waste, or rather who has the most choices about what can be done? The answer is not hard to find. It is business.

Considering the life cycle of a product from the manufacture until the end of its useful life, producers, material suppliers, trade, consumers and public authorities share specific waste management responsibilities. However it is the product manufacturer who has a predominant role. The manufacturer is the one to take key decisions concerning the waste management potential of his product, such as design, conception, use of specific materials, composition of the product and finally its marketing. The manufacturer is therefore able to provide the means not only to avoid waste by a considered utilisation of natural resources, renewable raw materials or non-hazardous materials, but also to conceive products in a way which facilitates proper re-use and recovery. Marketing, labelling, the issue of instructions for use and of data sheets may contribute to this aim.

FSC

Already the outlines of new and better approaches to education and recycling appear. First the real world possibilities

Extended producer responsibility becomes Focus No. 1. Also called 'cradle to cradle' production. It has been argued that this 'take back'of material or product adds to business costs and this will mean higher prices. A neat but somewhat flawed argument. Waste is never free – either the consumer pays via taxes for waste disposal or via a higher price. If the waste is uncollected the consumer and government also pay in health care costs. Wise firms soon realise that there is a financial incentive towards minimal materials use, minimal packaging and excellent design – including disassembly – if they are mandated to take products back.

Some waste does end up at home or school and someone has to deal with it. Here we need to compare and contrast the effectiveness of various **incentives and penalties** which promote waste reduction or the use of reclaimed material. There is an important role for schools here because the ground needs to be laid for changes which are going to mean an end to the 'bin it and forget it' mentality. In both 'cradle to cradle' production and waste minimisation or waste collection the role of **prices as messages** is central. Clearly the moral argument has failed to effect significant change – in the UK recycling rates are low while waste totals are growing steadily. Tactics in other places range from limiting the size of bin and taking only that free, to charging for all waste while separated material for recycling is collected free; to 'swap meets' where bigger items are given away or exchanged.

The consumer is really Focus No 3, bottom of the pile. Ahead of her is the government. Lester Thurow, an economist, wrote: "*The proper role of government in capitalist societies is to represent the interests of the future to the present.*" According to Jonathan Porritt this is a necessary and appropriate role. He says:

❝ *Most consumers in the rich world may claim that they want to lead more environmentally responsible, ethical lives, but only a small percentage of them actually do it. This gap has persuaded many companies that there is nothing to gain in designing and marketing goods and services for the 'wannabe-greens', because they don't really wanna be green all that much. Fine. But why don't governments get round that particular blockage by compelling companies to go green and ethical on behalf of the consumers who won't do it for themselves?* **❞**

Earth/Guardian Aug 22nd 2002

And another thing. Only governments can remove those huge world-wide and **perverse subsidies** which make the extraction of virgin wood, coal, oil and the trading of energy and products happen below market price let alone the real, or full, cost. How can small scale recycled material manufacturers compete?

So, way down the list comes the consumer. He or she too understands the importance of prices and considers various ways of keeping garbage costs down.

An ESD 'recycling' education programme now presents itself... if a little tongue in cheek.

Understanding...	In other words...
1. Extended producer responsibility.	"Why business matters most when it comes to waste."
2. How removing subsidies for new raw materials, providing incentives and penalties to reduce waste, mandating resource efficiency and ethical practices works.	"What governments do and might do."
3. Informed consumer choices.	"How do I keep my garbage costs down?"

Yes, it's a lot harder than 'lets collect tins' and 'think of a new use for yoghurt pots' but sticking with the cliches is worse. As JM Keynes noted: "*If a thing is not worth doing, it is not worth doing well.*"

Weblinks:

http://www.sydney.foe.org.au/SustainableConsumption/

Workshop tasks

1) Many educators do not understand terms such as 'extended producer responsibility' or 'perverse subsidies' or even' prices as messages'. How can these be made visible to educators and then to young learners?

2) It's possible to relate the Jonathan Porritt quote to the results of the Prisoner's Dilemma exercise (p. 103). Sustainability is beyond the rational action of individuals making decisions on their own – they rationally choose unsustainable actions. The role of society and business is crucial. Do you agree? Explain in terms of the Prisoner's Dilemma.

3) A colleague challenges you with "*What's wrong with collecting waste for recycling?*" What do you say?

4) Why is there no school known to the author or the FSCEE which practises this reworked priority or something like it in its curriculum?

Chapter 5
Sustainability and teaching and learning styles

❝ To teach is to learn-twice. When we understand something well enough to teach it, we can claim to really know it. **❞**

❝ ...reformers of problems in education often fail to identify and resolve the problem of education itself, because they do not recognize how education is also subject to a community of often implicit assumptions. **❞**

David Orr (1994) *Earth in Mind*

Although experience varies from country to country, there are some interesting pointers towards what might be 'good practice' when it comes to learning for sustainability. The most obvious is that a generally interactive learning style is consistent with a shift in world-view from the mechanistic to more dynamic models. We are not observers or passive cogs in a machine we are participants... therefore an experiential learning style is called for. The concept is simple to grasp. It is often described as an *iterative* or spiral model. It is about revisiting what we know and don't know. The familiar 'circle feeding itself' (opposite) is again the visual model most often used, although this time it is derived from the well-known work by Kolb and others.

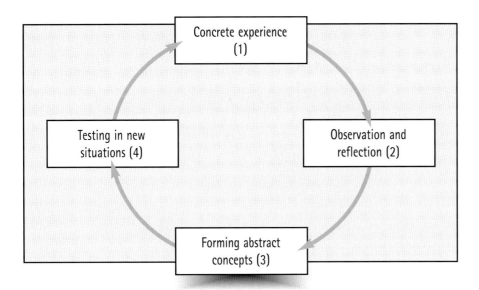

Much of the workshop and classroom material provided in this book has clear similarities with this approach. Another, related, model is based on the idea that all learners have pre-existing knowledge which needs to be clarified and challenged before it can be remodelled – before *learning* takes place. It is also a very useful guide to designing more 'active learning' type resources.

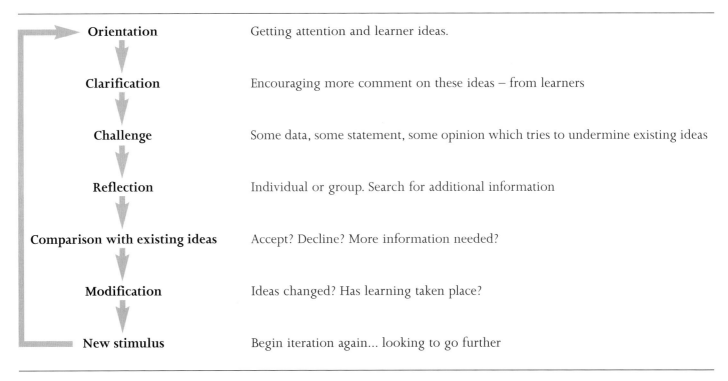

Orientation	Getting attention and learner ideas.
Clarification	Encouraging more comment on these ideas – from learners
Challenge	Some data, some statement, some opinion which tries to undermine existing ideas
Reflection	Individual or group. Search for additional information
Comparison with existing ideas	Accept? Decline? More information needed?
Modification	Ideas changed? Has learning taken place?
New stimulus	Begin iteration again... looking to go further

Source: 'Constructivist' sequence, based on original work in Leeds University

Orientation can be via a variety of stimuli – from text and data to poems, photos, objects, video, games, simulations and stories – anything which engages learners and prompts them to respond. Much of the process thereafter is through using and testing learners' existing ideas, getting them first to explain and clarify, without teacher criticism, then helping them to engage in a challenge to their pre-existing understanding (this might be other evidence, photos, data, experimentation, opinion pieces and so on) and again using their own work, and interaction with each other as far as possible, helping clarify any new learning. Perhaps by testing it in a new situation… and so on. There is a worked example based on some advertising copy from McDonalds in Appendix II (Healthy Choices p. 107) and online.

⅄ Workshop tasks

How far does the Healthy Choices exercise (p. 107) use the constructivist model (p. 71)? Identify the key stages in the process – and any missing elements.

It uses an example from consumer lifestyles to engage learners – but with bridges to the global situation. Is this always possible? Even the notes admit that some resources included are for higher ability learners.

How could the lesson be improved without losing the sustainability context? (Chopping off the difficult bits is not acceptable!)

Is the exercise fair – on its subject matter, on learners?

Does it matter that there is no obvious conclusion?

5.1

Many ways

Not forgetting that there are many kinds of intelligence as well as ways to learn.

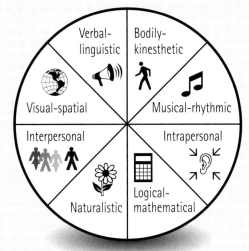

The theory of multiple intelligences was developed in the 1980s by Dr. Howard Gardner, professor of education at Harvard University. It suggests that the traditional notion of intelligence, based on I.Q. testing, was far too limited. Instead, Dr. Gardner proposed eight different intelligences to account for a broader range of human potential in children and adults.

These intelligences are:

Linguistic intelligence (word smart)

Logical-mathematical intelligence (number/reasoning smart)

Spatial intelligence (picture smart)

Bodily-Kinesthetic intelligence (body smart)

Musical intelligence (music smart)

Interpersonal intelligence (people smart)

Intrapersonal intelligence (self smart)

Naturalist intelligence (nature smart)

Dr. Gardner said that our schools and culture focus most of their attention on linguistic and logical-mathematical intelligence. We rate the highly articulate or logical people of our culture. He also said that we should place equal attention on individuals who show gifts in the other intelligences: the artists, architects, musicians, naturalists, designers, dancers, therapists, entrepreneurs, and others who enrich the world in which we live. Unfortunately, many children who have these gifts don't receive much reinforcement for them in school. Many of these kids, in fact, end up being labelled 'learning disabled,' 'ADD (attention deficit disorder)', or simply underachievers, when their unique ways of thinking and learning aren't addressed by a heavily linguistic or logical-mathematical classroom. The theory of multiple intelligences proposes a major transformation in the way our schools are run. It suggests that teachers be trained to present their lessons in a wide variety of ways using music, cooperative learning, art activities, role play, multimedia, field trips, inner reflection, and much more'

Source: Armstrong (2000)

Another factor in the selection or creation of appropriate teaching and learning styles is the very nature of sustainable development – its futures-orientation, its breadth, its controversiality and the uncertainty surrounding it. Handling this in a didactic or teacher-dominated manner is likely to be counterproductive if not completely absurd (it tends to generate dogma) whereas using an enquiry approach or one based on challenging tentative conclusions can develop insight, a respect for other viewpoints and values, and that ever-important 'critical faculty' (see learning models on p. 71).

Educators are participants in the development or adaptation of appropriate materials and not just as *deliverers*. One approach consistent with the idea of participation and 'active learning' is called **action research**.

It was first defined fifty years ago by Corey as "...*the process through which practitioners study their own practice to solve their personal practical problems*".

66 *Action Research is a fancy way of saying let's study what's happening at our school and decide how to make it a better place.* 99

Emily Calhoun

ⓘ 5.2

Why use Action Research?

Action research has been employed for various purposes: for school-based curriculum development, as a professional development strategy, in preservice and graduate courses in education, and in systems planning and policy development. Some writers advocate an action research approach for school restructuring. Action research can be used as an evaluative tool, which can assist in self-evaluation whether the 'self' be an individual or an institution.

Teachers participating in action research become more critical and reflective about their own practice. Teachers engaging in action research attend more carefully to their methods, their perceptions and understandings, and their whole approach to the teaching process.

Lawrence Stenhouse, a leading writer on the curriculum once said, "It is teachers who, in the end, will change the world of the school by understanding it". As teachers engage in action research they are increasing their understanding of the schooling process. What they are learning will have great impact on what happens in classrooms, schools, and communities in the future. The future directions of staff development programs, teacher preparation curricula, as well as school improvement initiatives, will be impacted by the things teachers learn through the critical inquiry and rigorous examination of their own practice and their school programs that action research requires.

To learn more
http://www.ericfacility.net/ericdigests/ed355205.html
http://www.goshen.edu/soan/soan96p.htm

Very often action research is a collaborative activity where practitioners work together to help one another design and carry out investigations in their classrooms. Research is designed, conducted, and implemented by the teachers themselves to improve teaching in their own classrooms, sometimes becoming a staff development project in which teachers establish expertise in curriculum development and reflective teaching.

The research study team provides support and a forum for sharing questions, concerns, and results. Teachers advise each other and comment on the progress of individual efforts. Engaging in collaborative action research helps eliminate the isolation that has long characterized teaching, as it promotes professional dialogue and thus, creates a more professional culture in schools.

5.2

The whole field of teaching and learning is vast and complex. Some writers tend to add up sustainability and good education and come to the notion that what matters is, primarily, 'learning how to learn', – from classrooms through to schools and beyond – that is *process* first and *context* (sustainable development) second. For sure, learning for sustainability can be a way in to extensive schemes, 'development frameworks', for schools but for many educators and learners alike discovering a sense of what characterises sustainable development and how it might be different or similar from what is learnt now is a more pressing need. If the context is not understood then the process is misapplied. And so a few very general 'teaching and learning' pointers to, say, a training day or workshop event now becomes visible. These are:

- **Big picture thinking**

- **Participation**

- **Continuous development**

Big Picture – it is to be based on a consistent and up-to-date model of physical and social processes: the emphasis is on a dynamic, fully interconnected and *iterative* world. If it has a bias it is towards connections rather than objects, wholes rather than parts.

Participation – in this dynamic model change can happen at any level and to maximise the chances of constructive change then, within enlightened 'rules of the game' (if possible!) educators will be encouraged to develop a range of learning and teaching styles...

Continuous development – ...and to meet their own professional challenges via reflection and action research.

Out of this process, and certainly not as a result of being handed down some detailed policy document, 'secure' institutional guidelines have an opportunity to develop from a very few guiding principles. 'Secure' because the practioners have used their classrooms as a testing ground for taking sustainability ideas into practice, they have, via action research, become informed, skilled professionals. More than this the initiative has become embedded, owned, important. They know what they are doing.

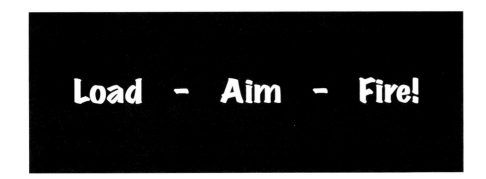

Chapter 6
Gearing up: some tools for ESD

There are three simultaneous challenges in providing frontline education for sustainability training events for educators:

• curriculum or *What we do*

• teaching and learning or *How we do it*

• the bigger picture (schools as institutions and actions by participants) or *How it fits.*

It is quite usual for people to expect new ideas to be presented in familiar ways, and more than this they expect new ideas to be essentially continuations, or variations of old ideas. They also want to be entertained. This makes the task of running ESD training a subtle game. Cooperation and support is being sought yet the work is potentially very challenging – philosphically, pedagogically and organisationally.

A 'run of the mill' education for sustainability training day can look like this: a session full of doom and gloom, about how ruinous a condition the planet is in; followed by some 'official' or UN statements about how important, therefore, is the idea of sustainable development. Nothing to disagree with so far but then comes something which can be uncomfortably like a sales pitch: how we should help young people build a better world (without being very specific what this better world looks like) as if it was very much down to the children ('our future')... and their hard working teachers of course.

It is all made convincing by examples of how spirited actions by young people have 'made a difference' to their communities, schools and the environment. Hours – if not days – of effort and struggle go into this kind of work up and down the country. This is not meant to be a confidence trick, but sadly it works out that way. A school with perfect grounds, no litter, a school which is saving energy and water through careful individual actions and even a long term commitment to community works will not bring a sustainable community or a sustainable school, it will just slightly moderate its unsustainability. The important (systemic) issues have not been addressed, let alone actioned. But the 'kicker' is this: who said *action* was a priority for schools anyway? The business of schools is education, which – on a good day! – means fostering understanding and drawing out, in partnership with the learner, what matters most and what matters least or not much at all and why.

One outcome from a refocussed ESD programme may be students who say that a school litter problem is not a major problem, and of passing interest only... or that water saving is best done through investment in simple technology and the regulation of suppliers, while energy saving is best done by the utility company charging a realistic price or... well? What *does* matter most?

In any event the conventional approach doesn't work, and it hasn't worked. Even in EU countries such as the UK, interest in environment and development issues among young people has *declined* – despite over a decade of widespread environmental education work and excellent exposure through the media – while indicators of overconsumption and waste continue to climb upwards. Yes, most young people are more *aware* of the problems but many actually *care* less. In Chapter 4 it was suggested that they learned that the school and society was not serious about the environment and that a few token acts would suffice, or perhaps they learned that a call for self sacrifice was easy to make but harder to do. Indeed they may have seen that the whole world seemed to be moving faster in other, more *interesting* directions.

A better way?

ESD workshop ideas in this book evolved over many years of experience. While still far from radical, they are hopefully challenging enough to present educators and others with the fuller dimensions of the work and dispel some of the commoner confusions about sustainability. However, they remain acceptable enough to give educators and participants alike an opportunity to get to grips with many important issues in an engaging and interactive manner. These ideas are only 'models', and display or *represent* one attempt at a very difficult compromise.

A training event cannot cover everything in the way that a dedicated university or distance learning course, or 'school development framework' on ESD can. Choices need to be made and the assumption below is that educators have a good knowledge of their own work, are interested in the classroom and learning and are professional – they seek to continuously improve their practice. If this is a useful summary then it is no surprise to find the training event biased towards two elements of our three identified areas – the *How we do it* and the *What we do*. Put another way, it uses a range of classroom or workshop examples to get to grips with learning and ESD. In the jargon it aims to support a 'grassroots professional development model' – it argues that a school can only confidently engage with ESD by **action research** (see Chapter 5) i.e. the 'planning-trying-reflecting-evaluating-planning' cycle. From this process sufficient depth of understanding and commitment emerges to enable the school to progress to a policy which expresses the best of what has been learnt in the action research and which teachers can commit to as it is scaled up to school level.

Sure this is an ideal, but it *is* consistent with the general idea in sustainable development of 'closed loops', of 'dynamic systems' and, in new models of how we learn; effective learning is also an *iterative* process and is particular to our own individual and community's circumstances.

Agenda 21 was also based on community self determination and it is another example of how sustainability can prompt reflection and revision wherever it touches. The alternative, of an imposed, detailed arbitrary policy on ESD which is mapped for teachers irrespective of circumstances goes against much of what makes sustainability generally and ESD in particular, potentially so exciting.

Talking through a day

Session 1: *A briefing on education for sustainability* (6.1-6.3)

Talking of compromise... this short briefing is great for managers or school directors who need to get up to date on the broad principles. It is useful for teachers too, of course and it takes the form of an *aide memoire*: a mix of diagrams and short statements around which the trainer develops a commentary. Only the laziest trainer sits there reading the briefing like a lecture, so please don't do it. An obvious point, but a trainer should be confident with the ideas behind sustainable development. The trainer has access to the whole of this book in order to be able to develop a suitable commentary and add illustrative material. Copies of the briefing could be used as a hand-out **AFTER** the session.

Time: 60–90 minutes, mostly discussion and comment.

Images can also be used as a stimulus to start discussion (see 6.4). These images can be used to get a sense of what the members of the group think about the state of the world and its prospects, about economy, society and environment.

The usual open-ended questions are 'What's this about?' or perhaps 'Part of the present or future?' 'Is this a bit over the top... or is there a fair point being made?' Additional ideas occur in the text below some of the items on p. 85-87.

> ### (i) 6.1
> **The briefing**
>
> The briefing is only a *characterisation* of where we are and what is before us with ESD so do not defend the statements too strongly if someone wishes to be a mite confrontational. The 'devil is in the detail' as always. The briefing is an over view to help develop discussion and is not meant to be dogmatic. The diagrams should help those who prefer a 'visual' learning style.

📖 6.1: Two contrasting views on sustainable development

View **A**

Key words
technocentric, accommodatory, centralised

Key books
Natural Capitalism (1999)and *Factor Four* (1998) (Lovins/Hawken)

- The 'world-view' we adopt shapes how we engage with the issue of sustainable development. The dominant world-view is still that of humans as managers of the earth alongside a reductionist, 'mechanical' view of how the world works.

- **Conventional perspective:** trends in environmental data and social data reveal major problems (see WRI /UN data) but faith in markets, trade and economic growth remains undiminished. Solution: "*business as usual but greener.*"

- **View of sustainable development:** *balancing* economic growth with environmental protection and social progress. In effect, still economic growth-led.

- **Method:** main thrust is *eco-efficiency* – using fewer materials and energy for each unit of output. Better waste management – recycling etc. Largely a technical solution with some regulation. Social progress is left to trickle down – as economies become wealthier we assume that the poor become less poor. 'A rising tide lifts all ships.' Globalisation of markets accepted and encouraged. Some use of price or cost incentives and penalties allowed.

- **Bright spots:** in near future, hydrogen cells, solar photovoltaics and cheap renewables combined with move towards zero emissions in industry. Minimal global agreements e.g. carbon trading, CFCs etc.

- **Role of education:** focus on *individual* awareness and small-scale community action especially regarding waste, energy and 'pollution'. Discussion of alternative political, social and economic approaches and priorities minimal. Does not question schooling or its aims. Changing methodologies in school acceptable – to some extent.

Note: some argue that environmental problems are not as bad as we think: see book *Skeptical Environmentalist* (Lomburg) and many US based lobby groups.

View **B**

• The 'world-view' we adopt shapes how we engage with the issue of sustainable development. Emerging world-view is that humans are just part of a complex system like the earth and its biosphere ('ecosphere'), not managers, and that there are potentially huge dangers in trying to manage it. Adopting a precautionary view and accepting limits to human interference and economic growth follows. View of how the world works is systemic, holistic, dynamic. Humans must work with, not against, nature.

• **Emerging perspective.** Trends in environmental data and social data reveal major problems (see WRI/UN data) and what is required is a rethink of what is meant by progress and how we achieve it. More is not necessarily better and there is a social justice argument which says that local not global development should be primary. 'The crisis of ecology and development changes everything.'

• **View of sustainable development:** a stable ecosystem and guaranteeing social justice are priorities before ill-considered economic growth. Economics serves the social and ecological agenda not the other way around. It can't be sustainable otherwise.

• **Method:** also accepts *eco-efficiency* is crucial but also sees enabling a plurality of diverse and devolved democratic developments as a priority. Quality of life not economic growth per se. Refined and broad indicators of progress to become central. Local rather than global emphasis. Prices of energy and materials, goods and services to reflect actual environmental and social cost. Taxes shift from people to materials, waste and energy.

• **Bright spots:** impact of this thinking spreading widely (new sciences of complexity and chaos support systems-thinking) and many valuable experiments underway e.g. eco-villages, Real Progress Indicators, parts of LA21.

• **Role of education:** actively questioning the status quo and exploring possibilities for the future. Accepts that individual action is useful but limited and that systemic change needs to be discussed. Questions validity of conventional schooling and methodologies for an ecological future.

Key words
ecocentric, systemic, radical, devolved

Key books
Planet Dialectics (Sachs) (1999)
Beyond Growth (Daly) (1997)

6.2: Some proposals

• ESD is **more** than environmental education or Nature education

• ESD, whether adopting a 'radical' or accommodatory view (or some mixed/inconsistent view) includes significant social and economic threads.

• Science-based teaching about Nature and how we should protect it is not, by itself, anything to do with ESD.

• Because of the 'call to citizen action' ESD is often taught through participatory methods. (Key terms include: active learning; groupwork; enquiry-based learning; democratic classrooms.)

• Many teachers are **not** confident with participatory methods and some actively dislike them. This makes ESD even harder to promote.

• Teachers and others request help in identifying just what sorts of work would promote ESD. Below are some key questions which reflect an approach consistent with ecosphere stability (**SEE**: sufficiency, equity, efficiency).

SUFFICIENCY recognising eco-limits	*'How much is enough?'*
	And shaped by that:
VALUES	*'What do we really want?'*
	... **only** then followed by:
EQUITY and EFFICIENCY	*'How can we provide ourselves with accessible goods and services at lowest overall* **resource** *cost?'*
	finally
CLEANLINESS	*'What should we do about waste?'*

Source: Based on work by Wolfgang Sachs and Alain Durning

Another **SEE**: Social, Environmental, Economic.

A less radical 'pocket guide' for finding ESD opportunities…

Any discussion about resource use can be a focus for ESD because it will have social and environmental elements. **If** *these are recognised and balanced with the economic elements in the discussion then it probably contributes to an education for sustainable development.*

Ecological limits	**E**	is the defining condition (world-view discussions)
Sufficiency • Equity • Efficiency	**SEE**	are priorities for ESD discussion
Social • Environmental • Economic	**SEE**	a checklist for balance

Characterisation of much current classroom work

Doomy	–	the world is in such a mess…
Moralising	–	be altruistic and 'save the world'
Individual	–	yes, **you**, do your bit!
Sustainability	=	a grey world of less, of restriction, of pious people. '…a lifelong celery diet' – Paul Hawken. 'No thanks' say the population.

Positive ESD might be characterised by work which is

Upbeat	–	look what's possible – real examples
Practical	–	what are the choices for society and economy? What's in it for me? (must be more than altruism)
Systemic	–	change is not just me but **us** (political 'us'). Local group, government policy, business practice, market reform
Sustainabiliy	=	a clean world of opportunity, inclusion and empowerment. A high and rising **quality** of life

Caution: knowledge amongst some teachers about 'eco-futures' is poor. Some possible new knowledge for teachers includes: Eco-efficiency, biomimicry, permaculture, eco-design and build, hydrogen cells, photovoltaic cells, incentivisation, ecological tax reform, social and ecological indicators, ecofootprints, waste hierarchy, 'perverse' subsidies in energy/agriculture/road transport, issues about genetically modified organisms. And so on… quite a challenge!

FSC

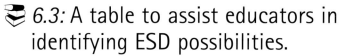
6.3: A table to assist educators in identifying ESD possibilities.

Key question	Changed thinking
Is this the REAL ISSUE? Do my lessons tackle the multi-dimensional nature of issues? Do they tackle causes and solutions as well as symptoms?	Think bigger picture – all five* dimensions of sustainable development (ecological, economic, social, cultural, personal). Think causes and solutions as well as symptoms. Think holistically. Think systemically.
Is this about NOW OR ALWAYS? Are my lessons FUTURE orientated? Do pupils get to consider probable and preferable futures?	Think sustainability long-term.
Do my lessons feature viable SOLUTIONS? Do some solutions demand less from the environment and allow access to more people?	Think sufficiency, resource efficiency, waste reduction. Think alternative technology. Think alternative economies of time and social welfare. Think social and environmental justice.
What is needed to achieve sustainable solutions? Do my lessons feature LEVERS FOR CHANGE?	Think technology, beliefs and behaviour, prices, markets, laws, regulation, planning, social welfare, media, lifestyles.
Where are the most effective levers for change located? Are my lessons realistic about POWER and SOCIAL CHANGE STRATEGIES?	Think individual, community, business, government and media at different scales (locally, nationally, regionally and globally).
Do solutions promote IDENTITY, DEMOCRACY and active and critical CITIZENSHIP?	Think rights of present and future generations and rest of sentient nature. Think environmental citizenship. Think how education can empower people to realise their common interest in sustainable development together with more fulfilling lives and identities.

* Huckle adds 'cultural' and 'personal' in his list of dimensions.

Source: Based on Webster, 2001 in *Education for Sustainable Development A briefing paper for the UK Teacher Training Agency* John Huckle

📖 6.4: Starting the day – some stimulus material

Source: Fiona Jacks

 A

New Zealand artist Fiona Jacks created this spoof advertising. Used on many roadside hoardings around Auckland in 1999 it prompted some passers-by to ring up a listed number and try and find out more about the product!

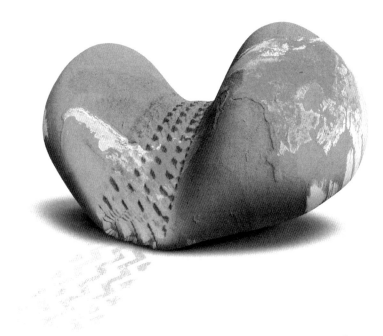

What was that bump?

Source: Adbusters

B

Are we careless about our world? Maybe we should be car-less? Lets take out the 'e' for excess.

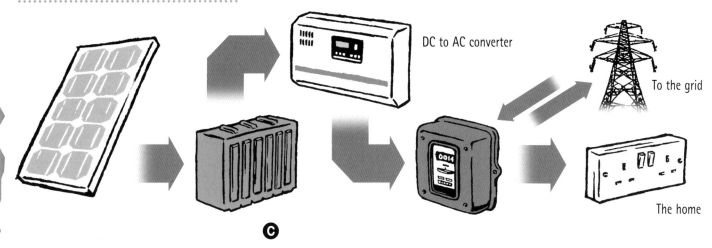

DC to AC converter

To the grid

The home

C

Is this the future – every house a solar power station, selling the excess to the grid?

REthink
REfuse
REpair
REduce
REuse
REcycle

D

Teaser: Education's job is surely at the top of this list of priorities in the search for a sustainable world. Some educators think promoting recycling – the least important strategy in this list – is enough.

Source: Basel Action Network
www.ban.org

E

What's the story? How does it read? Hmm...Recycling? Consumer excess? An end to old technology – hail the LCD and plasma screen? Dumping in less developed and less well regulated nations? Part of a sustainable future (or an unsustainable present?)

Coffee break

Session 2: **Lessons from Lessons**

This session is usually composed of a number of activities based on classroom work. The trainer uses the participants as her class (informally of course) and runs through the activity in a practical workshop setting. These activities vary and there are many examples throughout the book (and on line) to choose from e.g. *Sun or Shade* (p. 17), *Healthy Choices* (p. 107), *Trade Game* (if there is time).

The teaching and learning styles are to the fore in these sessions and if there is time for two or three activities so much the better. As a general rule try and use a variety of *stimuli*: using images, data, simulation, perhaps poetry and music or, where appropriate, information technology, and a variety of *techniques* (see Chapter 5) such as mind mapping, twos and fours, small group work, fragmentary information, brainstorming, judge and jury, field work, oral and written presentation.

Do not do activities for activities' sake. It should exemplify some of the aspects of the briefing and also show that ESD is accessible at the classroom level. Participants hopefully go from the session with an idea that 'this is OK, it can be done, in fact it is interesting.'

Time: 90–150 minutes.

Notes: Always allow plenty of time for discussion on what made this lesson different (pedagogically) from what students might normally do (a useful debriefing tactic is to break down what happened in the activity into **key ideas**, **skills** and **attitudes** and to ask participants to indicate what fitted under each category). A second stage is to debrief the sustainable development content. How is it different from what they might normally learn e.g. not 'recycling is a good thing' but 'what other choices might there be and how do we decide'. Not just energy *supply* options but 'energy conservation, demand management and good design'.

Lunch

Session 3: **Small Group Workshops**

Working in groups based on a subect specialism e.g science teachers, geography teachers, maths teachers etc., participants work on some tasks related to their own circumstances in school.

Task: *Discuss where SD potential is present in a relevant part of your existing work. Develop just one example of how you could amend your work in the light of what you have done today – or if you have experience in this area prepare a presentation on an SD related activity.*

In order to encourage 'big picture' or systemic thinking and get away from "*Here's the problem – what can you do*" the trainer can include a couple of prompts (see ⓘ 6.2).

Teacher groups make a presentation about their work. Usually the trainer will use other groups to provide a response first, based on statements such as... "*Would anyone from group 'x' like to ask any questions or make a comment on what we have seen?*"

Trainers need to be supportive. ESD is complex. Equally the trainer can seek further clarification and probe the understanding of the presenter and the group. Teachers usually use this session to get any complaints off their chests. These are mostly predictable, but all of them important and a serious challenge to the work on ESD.

ⓘ
6.1

ⓘ 6.2
Session 3 extra prompts

Prompt 1

...most environmental education has focused on 'green ' topics such as recycling, tree planting and 'nature conservation'. Connections have seldom been made between environmental issues and social, cultural and economic concerns. The underlying causes of environmental problems are rarely being addressed, as the primary focus has often been on dealing with the 'symptoms' of these problems (such as recycling waste). A lot of the focus has been on changing individual behaviours, instead of changing the systems that perpetuate unsustainable practices. Key principles of education for sustainability include critical thinking and social transformation. These elements have often been lacking from environmental education... this is probably because this kind of education is much more difficult to undertake.

Parliamentary Commisioner for Environment New Zealand

Prompt 2

Fundamental changes in the way societies produce and consume are indispensable for achieving global sustainable development.

World Summit on Sustainable Development

Prompt 3

While governments exhort their citizens to protect the environment through the slogan 'reduce, reuse and recycle', a huge advertising industry persuades people to 'increase, discard and dump'.

Clive Hamilton 'Critical thinking' a must?

Prompt 4

Prices are the most efficient information system; they largely determine decisions by producers and consumers. When prices do not reflect the full costs and benefits of production and consumption, the true facts about resource scarcity and environmental values aren't made known.

What proportion of our ESD work focusses on prices?

Perhaps the commonest and hardest question to deal with is:

a. *"This is all very good but where do we get the time to do it?"*

Other associated 'show stopper' questions include:

b. *"Don't participative approaches take longer?"*

c. *"What if the theme/topic is not here in the curriculum? How can I do it?"*

d. *"I'm only a junior teacher, my head of department/director isn't here so I can't say whether this can be done."*

e. *"Isn't this political. I don't know if we should consider this."*

Don't dismiss these concerns. There is no easy answer to any of them and the trainer will need to have considered her response to all of these well before the training day.

Some example responses to (a) include:

i. *"If developing skills and thinking are important then we need to find time… are you saying that these things are not important? Or maybe not as important as examination work?"* (Trainer can concede this point but questioner has been reminded that knowledge is only a part of schooling);

ii. *"Experience has shown that many students find these sorts of lessons more motivating …so students work with enthusiasm…"* (True…);

iii. *"It's a question of school priorities – if we don't find time then surely we risk teaching the irrelevant to the uninterested? After all the world is changing and schools surely need to reflect this change?"* (Again concerns of teacher are refocussed into a real world context and the teacher cannot argue for irrelevance… hopefully);

iv. *"Many schools find that work done elsewhere is repeated and not really progressed. How many junior (primary schools) do recycling and its supposed benefits for it to be done again in high school?"* (A sensitive issue but the lack of effective school communication often leads to overlap and waste);

v. *"How sure are we that teaching and learning are connected securely in the current approach? Just because we have 'done' a topic doesn't mean it is learnt? Time may be better used if teaching is more effective…"* (Using this argument can seem offensive to some and the use of the word 'we' is crucial in avoiding unhelpful confrontation).

Session 4: **Plenary**

Tie the day together so far. Prepare for this with some flip charts or pin up sheets carrying some key points which have emerged through the day. Ask participants if they wish to add any. Keep this session moving quickly as the end of the afternoon approaches. Use it to reinforce any key ideas and reassure participants that progress has been made, that ESD is possible and something to be enthusiastic about (see 6.3). This session leads onto action planning where participants make concrete plans for change.

Chapter 7 explores the wider institutional contexts and asks whether a sustainable school is possible.

Time: 20 minutes.

Session 5: **Action planning**

This depends on the aims for the day but the format is usually one of small group discussion to establish discrete actions: 'what?,' 'by whom?', 'using what resources?', 'by when?' – and to whom the outcome of the action will be communicated. A written, shared and agreed set of actions is the usual outcome.

(i) 6.3

Key 'up' points

- World is changing rapidly and educators have a responsibility to recognise this.

- SD is on the agenda – UNsustainability can't be!

- ESD can extend and also improve quality of teaching and learning as well as provide relevance.

- It can start anywhere in a school – a single lesson for example.

- Eco clubs and 'action' are not top priority anymore: it is worth mainstreaming into everyday subjects and schemes of work.

- Policy can follow from a period of experimentation and professional development through action research – so don't worry too much about it all now.

Session 6: **Evaluation**

A variety of styles are possible from detailed written evaluation to informal 'good things' and 'bad things'. The use of the material supplied in the action planning and the evaluation results might be very important to the project funders but also to participants. It is part of that iterative process – feedback is the key to a new cycle of learning and development.

Time allowed for Sessions 5 and 6: flexible, approximately 45 minutes.

'Y' *Alternative workshop task*

"There is something unbelievable about the world spending hundreds of billions of dollars annually to subsidise its own destruction."
EcoEconomy (Lester Brown)

Removing the $700 billion which oil, agriculture, forest and fisheries receive in subsidies is claimed to be one of the single most significant acts which could contribute to sustainable development.

Why spend another day on studying recycling or energy saving per se when one of the dominant causes of waste is 'inaccurate pricing'? Let us find a way of making this issue interesting and engaging. What do you think?

`Y` Finding the match

Here is an extract from a checklist produced by the international environmental pressure group Greenpeace which was used as a lobbying tool at the much criticised World Summit on Sustainable Development in Johannesburg (2002). It is a useful list, not so much for its demands but for its highlighting of key issues on sustainability.

Workshop tasks

Read and discuss the list and choose any five issues and how they are taught or could be taught in school. Some key words and phrases are underlined.

Greenpeace checklist for a successful Earth Summit

Climate and Energy:

• Ratify the <u>Kyoto Protocol</u>.

• Commit to new public finance for renewables: to bring clean, affordable, renewable energy to the 2 billion <u>people who currently live without electricity</u>.

• OECD governments commit to an immediate target of 20% of their energy sector lending and support via their Export Credit Agencies to <u>renewable energy</u> development.

• OECD governments commit to ensure that all International Financial Institutions they support commit to an immediate target of 20% energy sector lending for renewable sources, and a phase-out of support for conventional energy sources within 5-10 years.

• OECD governments set domestic renewable energy targets of 20% within 10 years.

• All governments commit to phase out <u>subsidies</u> to conventional energy sources, estimated at $US 250-300 billion annually, within 10 years, with a transition plan to ensure that developing country economies are not damaged.

• Immediately stop any proposed construction of new <u>nuclear</u> reactors.

Forests:

• Commit to allocate the necessary funds for ancient forest conservation and <u>sustainable use</u> under the Convention on Biological Diversity's Ancient Forest work programme.

• Immediate establishment of moratoria on logging and other industrial scale projects in all remaining large ancient forest areas and other forest areas with key conservation values until representative protected area networks have been established in accordance with the <u>Precautionary Principle</u>.

• Commit to implementation of immediate measures to halt ancient forest degradation and loss, and promote ancient forest conservation and sustainable use.

Genetic Engineering

• Give priority to agricultural practices that respect <u>traditional knowledge</u> and the environment.

• Implement a programme to preserve and protect <u>agricultural biodiversity</u>.

• Adopt a new instrument to prevent <u>patenting on life</u> and oppose the <u>WTO´s</u> TRIPS approach.

• Commit to allowing no irreversible <u>releases of GMOs</u>.

• Commit to public control of agricultural biodiversity.

Toxics

• Ensure <u>corporate responsibility and liability</u> for ongoing production and use of hazardous chemicals, and clean-up of existing <u>toxic hotspots</u> such as Bhopal.

• Ratify the Stockholm Convention on <u>POPs.</u>

• Ratify and implement the Basel Convention <u>waste trade ban</u> of 1995.

- Corporate commitment to <u>clean production</u> and products.

Oceans

- Moratorium on fishing on seamounts, deep-sea rides, plateaus and other areas of high biodiversity on the high seas.

- <u>Genetic Engineering</u> free seas – no intentional or unintentional releases of GMOs into the marine environment.

Disarmament

- Reduce military expenditure in favour of increased expenditure on <u>sustainable development</u>.

- New initiatives on <u>disarmament</u>, in particular in relation to nuclear weapons.

Other

- Agree that <u>trade rules</u> must be subordinate to environmental rules, and not the reverse.

- Commitments from all governments to ratify by WSSD, and ultimately implement, the <u>Rio and post-Rio environmental treaties, conventions and protocols</u> that they have not yet signed or ratified.

Notes:

GMOs = Genetically modified organisms

OECD = Organisation for Economic Cooperation and Development (rich nations club)

POPs = Persistent organic pollutants

WSSD = World Summit on Sustainable Development

WTO = World Trade Organisation

Chapter 7
Institutional and beyond

" We cannot restructure a structure that is splintered at its roots. Adding wings to caterpillars does not create butterflies—it creates awkward and dysfunctional caterpillars. Butterflies are created through transformation... "

" As complex learning systems, schools are far more organic and dynamic than linear. We, therefore, must design them to function less like clocks, and more like kaleidoscopes, and to do so, we must ground our educational transformation in the science of our times. "

Stephanie Pace Marshall, author of *Chaos, Complexity, And Flocking Behavior: Metaphors For Learning*

In a book which is fond of discussing 'the bigger picture', it would be wrong to end without a look at schools and colleges as institutions. Sustainable development, if it is more than just tokenism, will impact on education as surely as it impacts on the individual, government and business. It would be hard to imagine the alternative – a very sophisticated, sustainable business and civil society circulating around a schooling system more reminiscent of 1905 than 2005 except for some computers and solar panels?

This chapter briefly explores two aspects of the bigger picture: the prospects for coordinating ESD in a school and also the prospects for what has been called an 'eco' or sustainable school.

Coordinating and structuring ESD?

There have been many attempts to try and describe an overarching curriculum approach for ESD. In the UK cross-curricular themes appeared in 1989 – including environmental education – but soon disappeared from view. In 1999 seven core concepts were identified for ESD and appropriate activities described for different subjects, ages and abilities from 5-19. Only the most dedicated teachers and schools could work with it and it is now largely forgotten, outside of officialdom. There are many pressures on a curriculum and an external ESD structure can prove inhibiting rather than supportive. As Prof W. Scott notes:

"Only the most highly motivated will try to come to grips with such imposed, external frameworks, whereas all are capable of examining the various ways in which their subject can construe the human-environment relationship. Such an approach also avoids the trap of assuming a false conceptual consensus relating to sustainable development. I have argued strongly here for a within-subject approach to sustainable development issues in schools. However, I do so non-prescriptively, recognising that schools must do what makes contextual sense to them".

Source: Scott (2002) *Sustainability and Learning*

66 *We cannot just add sustainable development to our current list of things to do but must learn to integrate the concepts into everything that we do.* **99**

Source: The Dorset Education for Sustainability Network

Schools can continually review and revise their responses to sustainability through the subjects and this mainstream approach is arguably both meaningful and achievable. Over a number of years sustainability would become a normal part of the work of *every subject*. This is an important point because traditionally 'environmental' issues were dealt with in the natural sciences and geography while 'development' issues were dealt with in geography and perhaps citizenship. But sustainability is not primarily about science or geography, it is just a historical accident that it is treated that way. Scientists were among the first to raise serious questions about the state of the environment, especially in what is often called 'nature protection' but since sustainability encompasses social and economic issues there is every case for its inclusion in all social subjects. Its relevance to everyday decision-making argues for its inclusion in personal and health education, except of course that this latter area suffers from a low status and is often badly implemented.

Professor Scott again:

All "...*educators have four kinds of responsibility to learners:*

1 *to help them understand why a consideration of sustainable development is in their interests;*

2 *to use appropriate pedagogies for active engagement with issues;*

3 *to help learners gain plural perspectives;*

Source. Scott (2002) *Sustainability and Learning*

4 *to encourage learners to continue thinking about such issues beyond their formal education.*

In the circumstances, doing less than this seems neglectful; and doing much more suggests an attempt to indoctrinate, which risks rejection and disdain. A fifth responsibility, of course, is to keep an open mind oneself as to what sustainability is. The need is to stimulate without prescribing – and to use conceptual frameworks as support for learning, rather than as restraints on imagination and creativity."

Schools may therefore use guidelines as to what should be covered in an ESD sense but it seems that these should be open to review and flexibly applied. After all, this is consistent with a world-view which stresses movement and change rather than structure and 'things'.

Sustainable schools by stages?

Learning by doing is certainly a pedagogical winner, it is just the quality and value of what is learnt that has been most under review in this book – if it is to be labelled an 'education for sustainability'. Traditional in-school 'eco-activites' such as student organised recycling, or water and energy audits, litter picking and school grounds projects find their place, let us say, as a **Stage 1** or starter activity with the proviso that in mainstream school these ideas are probed and tested in the everyday curriculum. This is rather a big proviso as what makes eco-activities so attractive is often their 'bolt on' character.

What's it all about?
Eco Schools is a great way to make sustainable development a part of the life and ethos of your school. Designed to fit into the curriculum, it's an award scheme that gets everyone in the school community involved in making the school environment better.

An 'eco club' is not the sign of a sustainable school, and only the foolish ever made that claim, but then again a whole literature exists on more developed 'do it yourself' approaches to environmental education. A good example is the large and successful 'eco schools' scheme (see 7.2) but it is hard to argue

(i) 7.1
No end to the journey

Some challenges of sustainability to think about before calling a school 'sustainable'.

Activities are sustainable when they:

1. Use materials in continuous cycles.

2. Use continuously reliable sources of energy.

3. Come mainly from the qualities of being human (i.e. creativity, communication, coordination, appreciation, and spiritual and intellectual development.)

Activities are not sustainable when they:

4. Require continual inputs of non-renewable resources.

5. Use renewable resources faster than their rate of renewal.

6. Cause cumulative degradation of the environment.

7. Require resources in quantities that undermine other people's well-being.

8. Lead to the extinction of other life forms.

Source: Eco-Schools www.eco-schools.org.uk

(i) 7.2

The Eco Schools process

The structure of the Eco Schools process is made up of seven elements. A school must have gone some way towards implementing all of them before applying for an award.

The seven elements are as follows:

1. Setting up an **Eco-Committee** to take the programme forward

2. Carrying out an **environmental review** to identify problem areas

3. Creating and carrying out an **action plan** to set environmental targets and working towards achieving them

4. **Monitoring and evaluating** your progress in working towards your targets

5. Integrating your environmental activities with the school's **curriculum**

6. Involving the **whole school and the wider community** in your environmental activities, making sure you are generating regular publicity

7. Creating an **Eco-Code** that sets out the school's aims and mission.

Source: www.eco-schools.org.uk

for it beyond quite narrow limits as it often reinforces the fallacies of an approach based overwhelmingly on personal commitment and action. The greatest of these fallacies is the 'Southbound Train'. Schemes such as this can blind people to the fact that while they are talking up efforts at 'walking north' through the carriages the train is still headed south, carrying all with it. Eco-schools represents the conventional wisdom of environmental education, and it is safe in that it is uncontroversial, provides reinforcement to schools looking for good PR and to build school-community links, but sustainability is far too large an animal to catch in such a net.

'Eco schools' programmes do have much to contribute to the idea of building democratic processes by promoting self-help, problem solving and by ensuring wide participation in the controlling 'eco-committee'.

A **Stage 2** might be revealed in the widespread mainstreaming of ESD in the curriculum and on the practical side it is most often developed into an investigation, where appropriate, of the purchasing policies of the school. If Stage 1 was identifying the issues and taking some small, low cost practical steps then Stage 2 is about management accepting responsibiity for some of its financial choices. There is no sustainability without 'closed loops' (see p. 37) and purchasing eco-products and services is surely essential. Stage 2 is often a very acid test of a school and many fall at this stage, confronted by 'economic realities' or bureaucratic rules. In many countries decisions about purchasing are not taken in schools and the problems of moving towards a sustainable school are exacerbated. As a learning opportunity it is excellent as it holds up a mirror to both the profound and often absurd characteristics of our unsustainable world.

Source: Polyp

A greener world or a health and safety issue?

Further down the line, a **Stage 3** might be based on choices about *significant* capital expenditure: in the school building, in its heating, lighting and water systems and their control technologies. If it is done with sustainability in mind and targets are set and achieved with savings in the say, 50-60% plus range (as a target a 60% reduction by 2050 appears in the UK energy whitepaper) then this is an advanced school indeed. It may go so far as to include local renewable energies – wind and photovoltaics are popular in countries such as Spain and Holland. Eventually the process will encompass more and more new buildings and major retrofits. David Orr, perhaps the most well known educator in the sustainability field refers to 'the building as pedagogy', i.e. the message of sustainability will be within the structure and function of the building, much as it is now – the messages of the buildings and how they function is anonymity, waste and dysfunction.

Although there is a new and very welcome emphasis on 'greening' estate management, and green building in the UK school sector, it is not hard to see examples of this process being accelerated with a little imagination – as in British Columbia.

> **"** Sir Isaac Newton saw the universe as an orderly clock. Today, scientists describe it as a shifting kaleidoscope. Could this new metaphor hold the secret for the transformation of learning communities? **"**

Stephanie Pace Marshall

A **Stage 4** exists, although it is almost never spoken of... the idea that large centralised schools are inherently unsustainable. The environmental and social costs of getting there (transport), the energy and materials costs in running the school, and the social issues which sheer size bring all argue for smaller, local schools with wider community involvement, flexible uses for the building, flexible timetables and – when affordable – well-targeted information technology to facilitate such complex administration. A shifting kaleidoscope...

What is at stake here is how far the very *idea* of schools as we know them will be changed by the sustainability debate. It would be naive in the extreme to assume that a sustainable society which is faced with redesigning itself would retain basically 19th century industrial models of education and their associated buildings. Schooling is struggling as it is.

 7.3

Purchasing – a tough test

Example: Purchasing Green electricity. The choice is there. Fifteen UK electricity suppliers offer some form of 'green' energy. Find out the differences in what's on offer – on-line. Switch suppliers – online. Pay the premium – yes its more expensive but cost comparisons are available – on line. It's easy to do in an informed way.

http://www.ukpower.co.uk/default.asp

In fact, a class of 14 year olds could make a recommendation for the school.

'As recommended by Friends of the Earth and *The GOOD Shopping Guide*. Good Energy achieves the highest rating with both these organisations.'

Source: www.good-energy.co.uk

 7.4

British Columbia's schools retrofit programme

So simple its obvious – isn't it?

What could...
a) reduce energy and water use among target organizations by up to 18% and 24%, respectively;
b) reduce greenhouse gas emissions by up to 230 tonnes per year (equivalent to the emissions from about 38,000 vehicles per year);
c) generate up to $110 million investment in building retrofits and 1,100 person years of employment; and yield cost-savings of up to $34 million per year?

How?
Utility companies retrofit schools/colleges etc to best environmental standards. Schools pay *same bills as before until retrofit paid for* so "facility and equipment improvements were paid for by the utility savings they generated".

The BC government helped organise and approve schemes. It didn't pay for them. Its a win win win situation (people, planet and profit).

Source: http://www.greenbuildingsbc.com/retrofit/index.html

John Huckle noted "*Schools are modern institutions in a post modern world*". To the extent that change here lags behind change in society as a whole: schools and schooling remain a part of the problem more than a part of the solution.

" *The crisis of the environment... is symptomatic of a prior crisis of mind, perception, and heart.*" David Orr argues therefore, that this crisis, "*is not so much a problem in education but a problem of education.* "

This is the start of a completely different book (see note) and clearly the road to a sustainable school is long and difficult. In the current day at something around Stage 3+ to 4 schools might be able to justify using labels such as 'sustainable school' – in a playful and provocative manner, of course!

End note

In our day sustainability is still an aspiration not an outcome. In truth it has hardly begun to register within formal education. The UN Decade of Education for Sustainable Development which begins in 2005, will give a fillip but it is wider shifts in emphasis and concern in society, and business (let it be said) which are perhaps most hopeful. Things change and schools will follow along too. Witness the following little speech and imagine it being given in, say, 1982 – it would have been quite impossible.

"*The old energy economy that's cheating us as a planet is very well organised, highly centralised, rich as can be and very well politically connected. And the new energy future is decentralised, entrepreneurial and needs people like you to say 'Give me a clean car, give me solar shingles to put on my roof – give me a clean future'.*"

Who said this? Ex-President Bill Clinton

Notes:
See for example *Schools Out* a speculative piece by Caroline Walker and Ken Webster on the *Resurgence* website http://www.gn.apc.org/resurgence

It's not 'doing your bit' for the evironment but 'demanding your future in a clean environment'. An interesting change of perspective and change of venue as well, not a school or university hall but a speech about raising awareness of global warming given at the beginning of a Rolling Stones concert in Los Angeles.

Short bibliography

Sustainability

Natural Capitalism the Next Industrial Revolution. Hawken, P., Lovins A. & Lovins, L. Earthscan, London. (1999).

Factor Four Doubling Wealth, Halving Resource Use. Lovins, A. et al. Earthscan, London. (1998).

Planet Dialectics. Sachs, W. Zed Books, London. (1999).

GEO 3 (Global Environmetal Outlook 3). UNEP. Earthscan, London. (2003) includes CD Rom of data.

State of the World (2000, 2002, 2003). Worldwatch Institute, New York.

The Principles of Sustainability. Dresner, S. Earthscan, London. (2002).

The Total Beauty of Sustainable Products. Datchefski, E. RotoVision, Switzerland. (2001).

State of the World Atlas. Smith, D. Earthscan, London. (2003)

Sharing Nature's Interest – Ecological Footprints as an Indicator of Sustainability. Chambers, N., Simmons, C. and Wackernagel W. Earthscan, London. (2000).

Beyond Growth: Economics of sustainable development. Daly, H.E. Beacon Press, Boston. (1997).

Education

Sustainable Education. Sterling, S. Green Books, Totnes. (2001).

Education for Sustainability. Huckle, J. and Sterling, S. (Eds) Earthscan, London. (1996).

Greenprints for changing schools. Selby, D., Greig, S. and Pike, G. Kogan Page, London. (1989).

Multiple Intelligences in the Classroom. Armstrong, T. ASCD, Virginia. (2000).

Our Common Illiteracy. Jucker, R. Peter Lang, Oxford. (2002).

Earth in Mind: On Education, Environment, and the Human Prospect. Orr, D.W. Island Press, Washington. (1994).

Sustainability and Learning: what role for the curriculum? Scott W. CEE/University of Bath (2002). Download from www.cee.org.uk

Key Issues in Sustainable Development and Learning: A Critical Review. Scott W., and Gough S. (Eds). RoutledgeFalmer, London. (2003).

Ideas

Changing Consciousness. Bohm, D. and Edwards, M. HarperSanFrancisco, New York. (1991).

The Holographic Paradigm and other Paradoxes. Wilber, K. (Ed.) Shambala, London. (1985).

Suggested Weblinks

More data: Worldwatch Institute
http://www.worldwatch.org

Still More Data: World Resources Institute
http://www.wri.org

News and more news on the environment – US bias
http://www.enn.com/

Environmental Research Foundation (Rachel's Weekly)
Huge archive of informed commentary
http://www.rachel.org/

Global Issues That Affect Everyone – a link to another commodity, like coffee, which has very different rewards to different stakeholders. The banana. See also (http:- an efseurope URL for additional activity)
http://www.globalissues.org/TradeRelated/Bananas.asp

World Bank: Teaching and learning materials on social, economic, and environmental issues of sustainable development.
http://www.worldbank.org/depweb/

Poverty & Globalisation – Vandana Shiva
http://www.organicconsumers.org/shiva060704.cfm

Corporate economic clout
http://www.corpwatch.org/

David A. Cleveland on consumption
'U.S. consumption deserves reappaisal'
http://www.ia.ucsb.edu/93106/2001/archives.html

ESD

FSCEE manage the *efseurope* family of websites on ESD
http://www.efseurope.org

Many other examples of the author's work can be found at the WWF (UK) website **http://www.wwflearning.co.uk** and at Yorkshire Forward's Regional ESD site **http://www.yorkshireandhumber.net**

For depth and good conscience see John Huckle's ESD insights via **http://john.huckle.org.uk/**

Excellent perspective on ESD from New Zealand
http://www.pce.govt.nz/reports/allreports/1_877274_12_7.shtml

Appendices

(Also available online at www.efseurope.org)

Appendix I

The 'Prisoner's Dilemma goes *Green*' or 'Why we don't behave in an ecologically sound way'

Why is it so hard to bridge the awareness – action gap? And what has it got to do with ESD anyway? The classic game *the prisoner's dilemma* provides some crucial insights.

Play online...
http://www.princeton.edu/~mdaniels/PD/PD.html

Prisoner's Dilemma explained

In the Prisoner's Dilemma, you and Mary, an acquaintance, are picked up by the police and interrogated in separate cells without a chance to communicate with each other. For the purpose of this game, it makes no difference whether or not you or Mary actually committed the crime. You are both told the same thing:

- If you both confess, you will both get four years in prison.

- If neither of you confesses, the police will be able to pin part of the crime on you, and you'll both get two years.

- If one of you confesses but the other doesn't, the confessor will make a deal with the police and will go free while the other one goes to jail for five years.

At first glance the correct strategy appears obvious: neither of you confesses. But how do you know what Mary will do? You don't. The temptation to try for freedom is high. In fact the least risky decision as an individual, is 'defecting' (confessing). Maddeningly, Mary probably realizes this as well, so you both end up getting four years. Ironically, if you had both 'cooperated' (refused to confess), you would both be much better off.

So, what to do?

Sometimes it is better to get the tough stuff over with early so try this one: 'environmental problems can be characterised by general conditions'. In other, less academic words: 'It's the system, stupid!' These 'general conditions' make it very hard to transfer environmental awareness into ecological action because they are not open to any significant influence by the individual. It is important to explain why this is so, as it is arguably relevant to the success or otherwise of any and every 'education for sustainable development'.

Environmental resources can be called 'public goods', that is, an individual does not bear the costs of using them. This means that there is an incentive built into the system for each individual to use environmental goods and services while at the same time it is rational for them to avoid the costs of obtaining or preserving them. Moreover, the behaviour of a single individual is completely irrelevant as far as the overall environmental result is concerned. This means that the environmentally favourable results of changing individual behaviour are at best uncertain, while the costs of changing behaviour are quite sure.

The problem can be demonstrated quite elegantly in the prisoner's dilemma. The prisoner's dilemma is flexible as a game and here, in the enviromental context, it contrasts an individual's perspective with the collective and/or societal perspective. It looks like this: (see table) The individual (A) can act either in an environmentally friendly or an environmentally unfriendly way. The behaviour of others (N...) can also be described in the same way. The result is the familiar grid. If A chooses to be environmentally friendly and so does everyone else (N...) then see field **I** and so on...

Prisoner's Dilemma in environmental contexts

	Behaviour of other individuals	
	Env. friendly (Ecological)	Env. unfriendly (Unecological)
Individual Behaviour		
Env. friendly (Ecological)	I U 30 C 20 B +10	III U 0 C 20 B -20
Env. unfriendly (Unecological)	II U 30 C 0 B +30	IV U 0 C 0 B 0

Source: University of Muenster

Environmentally friendly (ecological) behaviour by society (other individuals) gives a personal benefit (U), which includes the decrease and/or elimination of health and other risks. Call it 30 units for each individual. At the same time the costs (C) of the change in behaviour that is required are 20 units for each individual in the society. These costs should not only be seen in terms of money, but also in terms of time, tasks undertaken, comfort etc. (B) is the net benefit or loss of the decision.

There is no doubt that in environmental education – as far as the ecological behaviour is concerned – field I is the most favourable one (everybody is behaving ecologically). But in most environmental contexts there is a systematic defect which restricts the achievement of this aim. This defect explains why the outcome in field I, which is desirable from a societal point of view, does not mean that a corresponding behaviour will also appear in reality. This optimistic expectation would only be well founded if the utility of 30 units for each individual strictly presupposes that one has to bear the corresponding costs of 20 units. But this condition is lacking in situations concerning public goods. If a public good has been made available nobody can be excluded from consuming it. This is even true if the consumers are not willing to contribute to the provision of this good.

The most advantageous situation for the individual is not represented by field I but by field II: A person can indeed increase her benefits (B) while refusing her contributions to an intact (or better) environment, while hoping that the other members of the society will bear the costs. This is the attractiveness of the 'free rider' position from an individual point of view emerging in situations concerning public goods.

The tendency to move from field I into field II is not set by individual values, intentions or knowledge, but is set by ... misleading incentive structures connected with the properties of public goods.

At field III you will see the danger of demanding an ecologically sound behaviour from the individual under those (misleading) incentive structures. A person behaving environmentally is not followed by the others and therefore has to bear the costs of 20 units without improving environmental quality. The prisoner's dilemma game rules that an individual is not able to influence the behaviour of the others. He/she remains exploitable. As those who act in an ecologically friendy way are exploitable and as nobody intends to play the 'moral fool' in the long run the result is that although environmental quality is desired by everyone it will not emerge. The predictable outcome is represented in field IV, even if everybody in the society would be better off under field I.

'Ψ' The Prisoner's Dilemma Workshop in action

Every person in the group is given two cards. On the back of one is a green circle and on the other card a red square. The first represents a choice to make an ecological action and the second a refusal to make such an action. It is explained that everybody will receive a benefit to their quality of life of 30 'units' if society acts ecologically. The personal cost of acting ecologically is however always 20 'units' – time, effort, etc. The group members are now asked to vote. As in the original prisoner's dilemma assuming everyone will act with others in mind (voting green) is a risky option.

Here are some outcomes of the vote and their possible interpretation:

a) Assume society is represented by the group.

If say 80% or more vote green and 20% or less red then overall we might accept position I in the table as the outcome. There are enough benefits to share but resentment must follow towards those in the minority who have received 30 units of benefit for no cost and are in position II.

If the proportions are reversed then clearly positions III and IV are relevant: the minority has put the effort in to no overall benefit (III) and the majority have done nothing and got nothing (IV)

b) Assume society is not the workshop group – keep fifty or sixty cards back.

Here the votes of the group make no difference to the outcome if the held back cards are revealed as all being either yes or no votes . Emphasise however the rationality of a 'no' vote if personal choices are being made which:

a – have significant costs – whether in time, money, effort or inconvenience;

b – are made in large anonymous groups;

c – have benefits which are uncertain, general and possibly long term.

This is exactly the case with most green initiatives e.g. Will you buy fair traded bananas? Research suggests that it depends on the personal costs being low.
(see http://www.fairtrade.org.uk)

Yes – (if the price is the same or very little more).

Yes – (if it's available where I go shopping).

Yes – (if the perceived or actual quality of the product is comparable).

In a re-run of the voting indicate now that the costs of voting green are reduced to 5 units and the benefits to 20. Does this change voting patterns. It should...

The original researchers of the University of Muenster conclude:
"the benefits of this model for the purpose of environmental education are that the dilemma emphasises the limits of traditional approaches in environmental education which mainly consider shortcomings in an individual's values as responsible for ecological problems: The traditional approaches expect a solution for environmental problems from changes in individual motivations. We can rely on this only in small group situations or when the costs of changing behaviour are low. The prisoner's dilemma can illustrate that this kind of environmental education tends to ignore the close connection between the incentive structure and the scope of ecological awareness."

This is especially true for environmental problems emerging in anonymous contexts (like individual decisions about getting around). Ecological actions are often more

FSC

unpleasant, uncomfortable and/or more expensive than their ecologically harmful alternatives. For those situations it has to be a basic task for environmental education to emphasize that it isn't just the individual motivation, intentions or values which are responsible for environmental problems but also the institutional framework with its misleading incentive structure. Accordingly, the challenge is not to seek ways to increase and spread individual morality but to change the direction of the institutional framework so that morality and incentives work in the same direction.' 'Good' eco-actions are rewarded and 'bad' ones punished.

Adapted from Univ of Muenster see http://www.uni-muenster.de/Umweltbildung/arbeit-e.htm

P.S. An exception to the rule which 'disappoints and deceives students'

In a setting like a family or a small community like a primary school, where people do not act anonymously, and, they are judged socially by their actions, it is possible to lead learners to whatever is being portrayed as 'sound environmental behavior' at that time. In the jargon, the environment has become a private good: within a small group of people (families, neighborhoods) it's not costless (anymore) to behave in an environmentally harmful and collective undesirable manner.

As a result some educators use this argument to continue the traditional programme – 'see, it works here!'

But can we expect to generalise what works for classroom experiences (small and familiar contexts) into anonymous social contexts? If educators don't ask this question the risk remains that environmental education disappoints and deceives learners. It is perhaps unsurprising that older learners often become cynical about the environment for as their intellectual development increases they are able to work more abstractly, to see the bigger picture and to sense that they have been misled about how the world works. An education which does not engage in the systemic does not educate at all, it deceives: quite simply different rules apply to the particular and to the general.

It is back once more to world-views: do you believe that the whole is more than the sum of the parts? If so, you will agree with the argument presented in this section, but change within schooling is also affected by 'general conditions' every bit as much as environmental matters and the awareness/action gap will exist.

"*What students can learn from the Prisoner's Dilemma is that a crucial point to environmentally more favourable results is not only the behaviour of themselves but above all the behaviour of those who can exploit the good will of our students, as long as there is no protection through changed incentive structures.*"

University of Muenster

Appendix II

'Y' Healthy choices? (Building ESD activities)

Theme: nutrition, healthy eating, corporate responsibility

Focus: science, citizenship, English and communication

Age range: 12-19

Background:

From February 3rd 2003 McDonald's in the UK sells just organic milk – Soil Association certified and GM free no less. There is a McDonalds nutritional calculator online. The consumer can be better informed about meal choices. There are also more healthy choices and variety in the McDonald's menu from this year. The consumer (i.e. me and mine) can choose to eat well and still have the convenience and service – and a good conscience. It's all about informed choice after all. Perhaps another moral in this story is that firms do respond to changing social trends and consumer pressure and that voting with the wallet can make the world a better place. So that's alright then?

This activity encourages pupils to consider whether positive personal choices can be an important part of social and environmental sustainability or whether they may be in conflict.

Aims:

• To examine the potential conflict between positive personal choices and social and environmental unsustainability.

• To contribute to pupils' understanding of what healthy eating means – including consumer information on nutrition.

• To promote critical awareness and thinking.

• To use web-based research and interactive online resources.

Weblinks:

Check nutrition levels at McDonald's:
http://www.mcdonalds.co.uk

Nutritional info for Burger KingUK etc:
http://www.burgerking.co.uk
http://www.bk.com

Discussion of change at McDonald's:
http://www.organicmonitor.com
http://www.organicconsumers.org/organic/hawken032403.cfm

McDonald's Report on Corporate Social Responsibility:
http://www.mcdonalds.com/corp.html

For a list of issues that McDonald's did not deal with in its Report on Corporate Social Responsibility:
http://www.foodfirst.org/media/press/2002/mcdonaldsissues.html

Preparation:

Familiarity with some current McDonald's advertising, especially menus, would be helpful (or some notes and observations from pupils' recent visits to the restaurant (if appropriate). A video tape recording of a McDonald's TV advertisement might be useful.

Resources:

II.1 McDonald's organic Milk advert

II.2 Extracts

Activity sequence 1:

A useful starter activity is to work as a class group and gather 'consumer' opinion in a very neutral way about McDonald's: about what individuals choose, about its popularity and its competitors for a 'fast food' experience. Carefully moving onto how healthy the choices are, collect opinions and adopt a position which suggests that consumers should be able to make up their own mind and that it is possible to eat healthily at McDonald's. Perhaps use the online nutritional calculator provided by McDonald's (see web resources) to compare and contrast different meals and options. This kind of online calculator is available from other fast food retailers (see web resources) and comparisons between brands and products is possible. In the context of healthy eating it is an opportunity to develop or practice pupils' understanding of standard terms such as protein and fat and the difference between saturated fat and 'other' fat. In an ESD exercise this detour into nutrition should be made to look like a major emphasis within an 'informed consumer' theme. Add in ▼ 1, an advertisement announcing that organic milk is standard at McDonald's. Is this a 'good thing'? It seems fairly obvious that it is. For reinforcement pupils use the McDonald's Report on Corporate Social Responsibility statement (see web resources) and add in other examples of positive change.

Ask pupils again how they feel about McDonald's and whether the business is changing in a positive way – as far as they are concerned. Taking their cue from the teacher, pupils can be expected to nod along to this proposal as they should do to a suggestion that 'careful personal choice matters'. Follow this with a dismissive comment along the lines of 'So that's alright then?'

Activity sequence 2:

Provide pupils in small groups with some additional material. Extract 1 is a news item on why McDonald's changed its menu and some of its practices. Pupils will discover strong commercial levers.

Extract 1

McDonald's, the international fast-food chain, has announced that it will start selling organic milk in its British restaurants from February 2003 onwards.

This was followed by news this week that the multinational reported huge losses of US$343.8 million in the last quarter of 2002. The company reported losses for the first time due to the closing of hundreds of its restaurants. The fast-food industry is suffering from intense price wars between chains, and a bad image due to outbreaks of BSE in Japan and Europe and the association of fast-food with obesity.

Source: http://www.organicmonitor.com

There are, however, objections of a more fundamental sort as well – and it is here that questions of sustainability enter the arena. (The earlier discussion is arguably pretty irrelevant to education for sustainability as it is so *partial* – it consists of looking at the consumer, the rich consumer and her selfish choices rather than the way that these choices emerge from the broader context).

An example of the importance of the broader context is found in the work of Paul Hawken (Extracts 2-4 and 6). Supplying these extracts should assist the debate around the challenge: 'So that's alright then?' Extracts 4-6 contain material at a higher or more difficult language level.

Pupils, depending on their ability might be encouraged to contrast the possibility of healthy choices for the 'selfish' rich consumer with the arguments that this can still mean an unsustainable and injust world.

Would they ask for further reform at McDonalds and if so, what?

Commentary

The essential contrast is between 'business as usual but greener/more efficient' – which is what McDonald's says it is attempting and the more radical position which says that business as usual is ultimately part of the problem. It matters a great deal to education for sustainability and how it is taught, for if it is taught primarily as a function of informed consumer choice, from the perspective of a developed world it is neglecting one of these two positions. Education for sustainability includes an exploration of alternatives and this means, *essentially*, ideas, philosphies, futures, not just consumer products.

66 *At this juncture in our history, as companies and governments turn their attention to sustainability, it is critical that the meaning of sustainability not get lost in the trappings of corporate speak. There is a growing worldwide movement towards corporate responsibility and sustainability, led in many cases by companies whose history and products have brought damage and suffering to the world. I am concerned that good housekeeping practices such as recycled hamburger shells will be confused with creating a just and sustainable world.* 99

Paul Hawken

Source: ©Ken Webster /WWF 2003 a version originally published as *So that's alright then? Consumer choices in an age of selfishness*

" And on that farm they have some cows that produce organic milk for all our restaurants. These cows have never eaten GM cattle feed, received routine antibiotic treatment or grazed in fields treated with insecticides, herbicides or fungicides. Which is why the Soil Association's stamp of approval appears on every single bottle. **"**

Source: McDonald's

II.2

Extract 1

McDonald's, the international fast-food chain, has announced that it will start selling organic milk in its British restaurants from February 2003 onwards.

This was followed by news this week that the multinational reported huge losses of US$343.8 million in the last quarter of 2002. The company reported losses for the first time due to the closing of hundreds of its restaurants. The fast-food industry is suffering from intense price wars between chains, and a bad image due to outbreaks of BSE in Japan and Europe and the association of fast-food with obesity.

Source: http//www.organicmonitor.com

Extract 2

Getting (McDonald's) to stop doing things they never should have done in the first place (buying antibiotic-laced chickens for example) is good, but that doesn't mean they are socially responsible. If I am hitting someone and asked to stop it, that doesn't make me a gentle person.

Source: Paul Hawken (1999)

Extract 3

In a survey of nine and ten year olds, half of them said they thought that Ronald McDonald knew best what kids should eat. And we know McDonald's is aware of the scientific and government data pointing to their food, promotion, and business model as being a cause of suffering for children and adults in later life.

Source: Paul Hawken

Extract 4

'Sustaining' McDonald's requires a simple unsustainable formula: cheap food plus cheap non-unionized labour plus deceptive advertising equals high profits. McDonald's recent sustainability report was a mish-mash of generalities and platitudes. A real report to stakeholders and investors will tell how much it truly costs society to support a corporation like McDonald's. It would detail the externalities – the societal and environmental costs not counted in corporate annual reports and accounting documents – borne by other people, places, and generations.

In McDonald's case, these externalities include: the draining of aquifers; the contaminated waterways; the strip-mined soils; the dangerous meatpacking plants where migrant workers are employed; the inhumane, injury-prone dead-end jobs preparing chicken carcasses for Chicken McNuggets; the global greenhouse methane gas emitted by the millions of hamburger cows in feedlots; the impact of their $2 billion advertising and promotional campaigns to convince young people to demand their food; the ethics of using toys and dolls to induce girls and boys into their restaurants. The list is longer than this. Unless the core values of the company are to nourish and protect children, you cannot make the supply chain socially responsible because the final outcome is destructive to life. McDonald's should not be sustained by people thinking their money, placed in Socially Responsible Investment funds, is going to a good cause. McDonald's recent initiatives, which you think make them socially responsible, are best described by Henry Thoreau as "*improved means to an unimproved end.*"

Source: Paul Hawken

Extract 5

McDonald's has an impressive record of responsiveness to our concerns. They responded on the beef sourcing issue, and annually reassert that they do not purchase beef from rainforest lands. They responded to concerns on the chicken sourcing issue, forcing a sweeping change in the way chickens are farmed, as farmers were forced to comply with McDonald's stricter standards. They responded to Domini Social Investments on the sweatshop issue, inviting concerned shareholders to work with them towards strengthening their social compliance programs, and their level of public accountability. As a result of this dialogue, McDonald's has produced its first public reports describing how it works to ensure that the products it sources are produced in decent working conditions. None of this makes McDonald's a pure, 'socially responsible company.' It is strong evidence, however, that McDonald's is responsive to these concerns and is doing a better job addressing them than many of its competitors.

Source: Amy Domini, Founder and CEO, Domini Social Investments

Extract 6

So what gives? What does socially responsible investing mean? Is it a way for upper middle class people to launder their money?... It seems to me that the first thing we have to look at is the business model if we are to determine whether a company is socially responsible. Getting kids hooked on junk food doesn't qualify. If the business model is corrupt, then it hardly matters if a company uses recycled paper or provides daycare. It is not just what we do, e.g. sell organic foods, but how we do it. In fact, what we do always comes from how.

Source: Paul Hawken

Appendix III

Five reasons why green consumerism is no solution

Here are five reasons why the environment has failed to become a mainstream market force:

1. There's no mandate. Though polls tell us that most consumers prefer greener products, the polls are misleading: they fail to ask the right questions. If you pose a question as a green-versus-ungreen choice... the answer is obvious: everyone prefers the greener choice. But if you probe deeper into consumer attitudes, the real answer is that consumers will choose the greener product – IF it doesn't cost more …comes from a brand they know and trust... can be purchased at stores where they already shop... doesn't require a significant change of habits to use... and has at least the same level of quality, performance, and endurance as the less-green alternative.

That's a high hurdle for any product. No wonder mainstream consumers are turned off to environmentally-conscious shopping.

2. The public is dazed and confused. Shopping with Mother Earth in mind is no mean feat, even for the most savvy of shoppers. After all, understanding the environmental implications of something as simple as paper versus plastic shopping bags requires digesting a fair amount of science, some of which is inconclusive, contradictory, or simply arguable. Both, after all, come from limited, declining resources, can be made from recycled material, and can be recycled. Which is better? Even the scientists don't agree. (Of course, the greenest bag is the reusable organic cotton or hemp bag you use thousands of times before it must be turned into compost, but that notion rarely gets considered at the end of a checkout line.)

3. People lack perspective. Similarly, most people don't have a clue about the relative environmental impacts of the things they do every day. For example, a good many self-described 'green

consumers' don't seem to find irony in jumping into their poorly tuned, gas-guzzling sport-utility vehicles with a cold engine and underinflated tyres to drive a couple miles out of their way in bumper-to-bumper traffic in order to purchase their favourite brand of recycled paper towels. Will buying the right laundry detergent or ice cream make the world safe for petrol-powered lawn mowers, leaf blowers, and chain saws? You decide.

The whole notion of green consumerism unwittingly contributes to this lack of perspective. It implies that greener purchases can help 'save the earth.' The dirty little secret of green consumerism is that we're not likely to shop our way to environmental health.

4. Companies making greener products are afraid to speak up. With good reason. Those early purveyors of 'degradable trash bags' and 'ozone-friendly aerosols' got their wrists slapped, so marketers are understandably shy on making environmental claims, particularly those that are scientifically debatable. And most companies aren't environmentally pure, so to call attention to one's green goods risks calling attention to one's ecological skeletons. Better to keep one's corporate mouth shut, right?

5. Green benefits aren't always evident. …many environmental initiatives companies take don't show up on product labels. For example, Anheuser-Busch saves millions of pounds of aluminium a year by shaving a few millimetres off the diameter of its beer cans, though they don't put eco-labels on cans of Busch and Bud. Nonetheless, they're having a significant impact when you consider the energy and resource inputs of aluminium, and the energy savings from trucking lighter-weight cans. It's certainly a greater environmental contribution than that of consumers pondering 'paper versus plastic'.

from Joel Makower http://www.organicconsumers.org/Organic/greenism.cfm

☝ *Workshop task*

In the light of this perspective from a more consumer-orientated country (USA) what do we say to children here about choices?

Appendix IV

Sustainable development – how then should we move forward?

'Y' *Workshop task*

Schools might use this list as a guide to the real, priority issues for sustainability which need addressing in any comprehensive ESD programme. Highlighted are the transitions and some key phrases. The challenge is how to make these adult ideas into student-friendly activities.

Sustainable development
How then should we move forward?

Adapted from Prof Gus Speth's notes*

I believe (May 2002) there are seven dimensions where progress, indeed transformation, is necessary to achieve sustainability. They address directly the underlying drivers of large-scale environmental deterioration.

1. The need for an early demographic transition to **a stable world population**. Here there is definite progress. The main need here is adequate funding for the United Nations' Cairo Plan of Action, which is being underfunded by half.

2. The second transition is to **a world without mass poverty**, where the prospects for widely shared prosperity are good. Environmentally the poor have no choices other than to lean too heavily on a declining resource base. But we also need this transition because the only world that works is one in which the aspirations of poor people and poor nations for fairness and justice are being realized. Eliminating large-scale poverty is no longer an impossible dream. It could be accomplished in the lifetimes of today's young people. Achieving these goals is problematical due to limited development assistance, compounded by protectionist trade regimes, social instability and corruption and heavy debt burdens.

3. The third transition is a transition in technology to **a new generation of environmentally benign technologies**. We need a worldwide environmental revolution in technology. The only way to reduce pollution and resource consumption while achieving expected economic growth is to bring about a wholesale transformation in the technologies that today dominate manufacturing, energy, transportation and agriculture. The good news here is that across a wide front, technologies that would bring about a vast improvement are either available or soon can be. Transformation of the energy sector must rank as the highest priority.

4. The fourth transition is a market transition to a world in which **prices reflect the full environmental costs**. The needed revolution in technology and the equally needed changes in consumption patterns will not happen unless there is a parallel revolution in pricing. The corrective most needed now is environmentally honest prices. Full cost pricing is everywhere thwarted today by the failure of governments to eliminate environmentally perverse subsidies (estimated globally at $1.5 trillion) and to ensure that external environmental costs are captured in market prices.

5. The fifth transition is a **transition in consumption** from unsustainable patterns to sustainable ones. Here, one very hopeful sign is the emergence of product certification and green labeling and public support for it. This trend started with the certification of wood products as having been produced in sustainably managed forests and has now spread to fisheries and to building design. Increasingly, consumers are voting green in the marketplace, and that is driving change. Another hopeful sign is the **new legislation in Europe and Japan** requiring that consumer durables be recycled; some require that manufacturers take back their products when use is finished.

FSC

6. The sixth transition is **a transition in governance**. The World Business Council for Sustainable Development has sketched several broad paths in environmental governance.

a. FROG – First Raise Our Growth. Let's solve our economic challenges first, it says. FROG is a business as usual scenario, leading to huge environmental costs, social inequity, and often social instability. It is a failure scenario, even in the eyes of business leaders.

b. GEOPolity – people turn to government to focus the market on environmental and social ends and rely heavily on intergovernmental institutions and treaties. Its record has been poor.

c. JAZZ – like the music, a world of unscripted initiatives, decentralized and improvisational. There is abundant information about business behaviour; good conduct is enforced by public opinion and consumer behaviour. Governments facilitate; NGOs are very active; business sees strategic advantage in doing right thing (see notes).

7. A transition in culture and consciousness. Clearly we need new habits of thought, a new world-view. The potential for conscious evolution is evident in great social movements that societies have already experienced, such as the abolition of slavery and the civil rights movement. It is possible that we are seeing the birth of something new – a change of consciousness – in the anti-globalisation protests, in the far-reaching and unprecedented initiatives being taken by some private corporations, in the growth of NGOs and their innovations, in scientists speaking up and speaking out, and in the outpouring of environmental initiatives by the religious community. We must certainly hope that something new and vital is afoot. And, ironically, what may drive this consciousness as much as anything else is the reality of our role in climate change.

There are hopeful signs, but to be honest we must conclude that we are at the early stages of the journey to sustainability.

*Source: Adapted from Prof James Gustave Speth 's May 2002 paper *The Failure of Green Governance*. Prof Speth, a Yale professor was a prime mover in the creation of the World Resouces Institute

Notes:

GEOPolity can be redesigned for success by insisting on new norm-setting procedures and new institutions, including a World Environment Organization. The case for an effective WEO is as strong as for an effective WTO. The international community knows how to create plausible multilateral arrangements and has often done so in other, mostly economic, areas.

Upscaling JAZZ – JAZZ is the most exciting arena for action today, with an outpouring of bottom-up, unscripted initiatives from business, NGOs, governments, and others. Seven large companies – DuPont, Shell, BP Amoco, Alcan among them – have agreed to reduce their CO_2 emissions 15% below their 1990 levels by 2010.

Indeed, Alcoa is reported to be on track to reduce its emissions 25 percent below 1990 levels by 2010, and DuPont is on schedule to reduce emissions by 65%. Eleven major companies – DuPont, GM, IBM among them – have formed the Green Power Market Development Group and committed to develop markets for 1000 megawatts of renewable energy over the next decade.

Home Depot, Lowes, Andersen and others have agreed to sell wood (to the degree it is available) only from sustainably managed forests certified by an independent group against rigorous criteria. Unilever, the largest processor of fish in the world, has agreed to the same regarding fish products.

NGOs had important roles in forging these corporate initiatives. They are the real maestros of JAZZ. Local governments, universities and other entities have also contributed. Over 500 local governments have now joined a campaign to reduce greenhouse gas emissions.